Chapter 1

Introduction to the Disneyland Resort:

The Disneyland Resort was officially unveiled on July 17th, 1955 by Walter
Elias Disney himself. As Walt Disney welcomed his first guests he told them:

> *"To all who come to this happy place; welcome. Disneyland is*
> *your land. Here age relives fond memories of the past, and here*
> *youth may savor the challenge and promise of the future.*
> *Disneyland is dedicated to the ideals, the dreams, and the hard*
> *facts that have created America, with the hope that it will be a*
> *source of joy and inspiration to all the world."*

Sixty years later, the Disneyland Resort still provides "joy and inspiration",
and now it is bigger than Walt could ever have imagined. There are now two
theme parks, instead of just one – Disneyland Park (the original, opened in
1955) and Disney California Adventure (opened in 2001). The resort also has
an entertainment district known as Downtown Disney with dining locations,
shops, a movie theater and more. For visitors looking for a magical stay, they
need look no further than the three on-site Disney hotels. Since 1955, the
Disneyland Resort has welcomed more than 700 million guests.

The original Disneyland Park inspired the creation of Disney theme park
resorts around the world, and even a hugely successful cruise line. It is
incredible how faithful to the original the company has kept Disneyland Park,
even 60 years later, while still managing to make it attractive to new families
and generations with updated technology, characters, attractions and shows.

In order to take in all the Disneyland Resort has to offer it will require a stay of multiple days. As a general guide, if you want to visit both parks and experience a small sampling of the rides and shows, you can do this in one day. For a more relaxed and enjoyable stay we recommend a minimum of two full days to tour Disneyland Park plus one full day for Disney California Adventure. Downtown Disney can be "seen" in an hour or so in the evening, preferably after the parks close.

Therefore, a stay of 3 full days should be adequate to see all the major attractions provided you follow the tips and tricks in this book. An ideal stay would consist of 4 to 5 days, allowing you to take in the parks at a more relaxed pace, watch the entertainment on offer, go back to your hotel for a few hours each day and even take in extra activities such as a spa session at the Grand Californian Hotel.

There has never been a better time to visit the Disneyland Resort. In 2016, the Disneyland Resort continues its 60th anniversary 'Diamond Celebration' which began in 2015. The celebrate will run until September 5th, 2016. For this celebration, Disney has spruced up classic rides such as Peter Pan's Flight, Haunted Mansion and the Matterhorn Bobsleds with new effects, as well as the addition of three brand new nighttime spectaculars that cannot be missed. Countless other touches throughout the resort will make your vacation even more magical. Now, it is time to begin to explore!

Disney lingo:

For the purposes of brevity, acronyms are sometimes used in this guide. Here they are in full:

Attraction – The general term for a ride or show.
Cast Member (CM) – A Disney employee.
Character dining – A meal where select Disney characters make appearances and visit every table to meet guests, sign autographs, take photos and make memories.
DCA – An acronym for Disney California Adventure park, the second and newest theme park at the Disneyland Resort. The park is also sometimes referred to as 'California Adventure'.
Disney Resort – A Disney hotel. This is called a resort because of its elaborate theming and the numerous amenities on offer.
Downtown Disney – The shopping, dining and entertainment district located just outside the Disneyland Resort theme parks.
FastPass – A free service to save you time waiting in line. Be sure to see our chapter dedicated to it.

Table of Contents

Guest – You, the person entering the theme park – you are not a mere visitor, but a guest!

Off-property – Everything outside of Disneyland Resort's land.

On-property – Everything that is within Disneyland Resort.

Queue – Sometimes this is called a "queue", sometimes a "line", sometimes a "queue line". They all mean the area you wait in before boarding an attraction, entering a restaurant, meeting a character or watching a show.

Quick Service – This refers to dining and means 'fast food'.

Standby Line – The regular queue for guests not using FastPass, where guests stand in line until they reach the front and experience the attraction.

Table Service – Dining where a server brings food to your table.

The importance of planning:

A visit to the Disneyland Resort *needs* to be planned. We will tell you that outright. Imagine going on a vacation abroad and not knowing what you wanted to see, not having an idea of where things are, or without having a map. Very simply, most people would not do this. Why do some guests do this at a theme park? Theme parks are where making the wrong decision can cost you an extra few hours of queuing.

A visit to the Disneyland Resort should be planned. You do *not* need to plan what you are doing every single moment of every day – this is a vacation after all. If, however, you *do* want to maximize your time in the parks, then make sure to follow our touring plans where the time you invest really pays off in short waits, and experiencing more attractions.

Military-style planning aside, every guest should have some knowledge of the following:
- Where are you staying? A hotel, a motel, on-site, off-site, or an apartment rental?
- How do you get from your accommodation to the theme parks? Is it a case of walking or taking a shuttle or a public bus?
- How long will I stay? What tickets do I need?
- What kind of food do you want to eat? Theme park-fare? Fine dining? Quick service? Table service? Character buffets?
- How long do you want to stay in the parks? A half-day, or until the evening?

You should also make sure to have copies of the maps to both theme parks. We have had some created exclusively for this guide book – they can be found at the end. You should use these maps to circle the the rides, shows and attractions you would like to experience with the help of this guide book.

Answering these questions will hopefully make you realize how crucial planning is. Start off by writing down the basics for each day and then you can 'go with the flow' from there onwards.

Can a trip to Disneyland be done spontaneously? Yes. Will you spend extra hours waiting in queue lines if you have done no preparation? Absolutely. Will you miss out on some hidden gems by not reading this guide? You will.

The answer is simple – read this guide in full, create a rough day-to-day plan, and get excited for your visit. We will undoubtedly steer you in the right direction, and your trip will be unforgettable.

Keeping up to date:

Visit our website at **www.independentguidebooks.com/disneyland** where we publish Disneyland information, such as ride closures throughout the year. For more information, seen our on Facebook at **www.facebook.com/independentguidebooks** and follow us on Twitter at **www.twitter.com/indepguides**.

Our email newsletter sign-up can be found on the right hand side of our website's main page – we only send out a handful of updates every year, but we make sure they are useful. Finally, if you have any questions, suggestions or feedback, use the 'Contact Us' section of our website to get in touch.

Limit of Liability and Disclaimer of Warranty:
The publisher has used its best efforts in preparing this book, and the information provided herein is provided "as is." Independent Guides and the author make no representation or warranties with respect to the accuracy or completeness of the contents of this book and specifically disclaims any implied warranties of merchantability or fitness for any particular purpose and shall in no event be liable for any loss of profit or any other commercial damage, including but not limited to special, incidental, consequential, or other damages. Please read signs before entering attractions, as well as the policies of any companies used. Prices are approximate and fluctuate.

COPYRIGHT NOTICE:

Chapter 2

Planning your trip

As we have already said in the introduction, planning your vacation to the Disneyland Resort is important, but it can seem like a daunting task. Follow these bullet points and you will be well on your way to a fully planned trip:

• Decide whether you will be visiting the resort more than once in the next year. If you will be, then consider getting an annual passport instead of buying park entry tickets. There is more information on annual passes in the **tickets** section. If you are a local resident, an annual pass almost always makes sense, provided the blockout dates work for you.

• Decide whether you want to stay on-site or off-site. On-site packages mean you get a hotel and park tickets all for one price. Off-site usually means that you pay for the hotels and park tickets separately, and stay at a non-Disney hotel. The latter usually works out significantly cheaper but you do lose some of the Disney charm by staying off-site.

• Get maps before you go – This guide book includes specially commissioned maps of both theme parks at the end. Combine these with our guide to the parks and decide which attractions you want to do. Then note down where they are on the map before you get to the parks. This is essential to making the most of your time whilst you are there.

• Check the opening hours of the park - The latest hours are available at **https://disneyland.disney.go.com/calendar/**.

• The Disneyland Resort closes rides for refurbishment and construction throughout the year. This is because the park is open every day of the year and annual maintenance is essential. The Resort tries to do this during the less busy seasons but some closures do require more time. Check which attractions are closed before booking to avoid disappointment at **www.independentguidebooks.com/dl/refurbs**.

• Download the Times Guide - Know when the parades and shows are taking place, and when the characters are set to appear. The schedule for your trip can be seen several weeks in advance here: **https://disneyland.disney.go.com/calendar/**. Once inside the park pick up a paper Times Guides for an easy-to-read summary.

• Read through the whole of this guide thoroughly, taking note of any key tips and facts you encounter.

• Check **www.independentguidebooks.com/disneyland/** for updates before leaving.

• Do not forget to pack mains adapters if you are not from the US as plug sockets in the US differ from others worldwide.

• If you are travelling internationally, buy your dollars before you get there or use a currency conversion card for the best rates.

Chapter 3
Getting there

There are many options to consider when traveling to the Disneyland Resort.

Driving:

If you are driving into the Disneyland Resort be aware that, unlike the Walt Disney World Resort, the Disneyland Resort is located in the middle of a town. Despite this, it is still the biggest tourist destination on the West Coast and therefore it is well signposted.

If you are navigating with maps or GPS devices the address of the resort is:

DISNEYLAND
1313 Harbor Blvd. P.O. Box 3232
Anaheim, CA 92803-6161

You will need to follow local signs to the Mickey & Friends Parking Structure (Disneyland Parking) when you are near the Disneyland Resort, as the address above won't take you there directly. Once parked, you can then board a complimentary tram from the parking structure to Downtown Disney and the theme parks. Only collapsible/foldable strollers are allowed on the tram. If you do not have one of these, the walk from the parking structure to the theme parks is approximately 1 mile.

You can use the same tram to return to your vehicle after visiting the theme parks. Parking is charged at $18 per day for a car. The cost is $23 for RVs and $28 for buses and coaches.

Alternative surface level parking is available at the Toy Story lot on Harbor Boulevard. Guests parking here will be shuttled to the Disneyland entrance plaza. Standard parking charges apply.

From the LA Union station area to Disneyland Resort it is a 30-minute drive during low traffic (26 miles) of which most of the journey (25 miles) is on the I-5 South. During heavy traffic this journey can take 60 minutes or longer.

Flying:

There are three main airports that you should consider when flying in to the Disneyland Resort. By proximity (closest first), these are: John Wayne Airport (SNA), Long Beach Airport (LGB) and Los Angeles International Airport (LAX).

John Wayne Airport (SNA):

Follow the signs within the airport to the Ground Transportation Center (GTC). The GTC is located on the lower level (Arrivals) of the East Parking Structure and is a short walking distance from all baggage claims and is well signposted. Once you reach the GTC, your options include:

- **Disneyland Resort Express** – This shuttle service provides direct access to the Disneyland Resort and several local area hotels. It picks up from in front of the ticket booth in the GTC area. This service is not run by Disneyland; it is run by Grayline Anaheim. There are hourly departures from 8:30am to 7:00pm. Fares are $20 each way and $35 round-trip for adults. There is often a promotion where children (under 12) go free with fare paying adults. Children's tickets are usually priced at $15 each way or $26 round-trip. Travel time to the Anaheim Resort Area is approximately 30 minutes, depending on traffic. Visit **www.graylineanaheim.com** for more information.
- **Taxis and shuttle services** – These are also available from the GTC. Ask about pricing, as it may be a more convenient and affordable option for larger groups than the Disneyland Resort Express.

Driving:

It is a 20-minute drive from the airport to the Disneyland Resort. Follow CA-55 North for approximately 2 miles from the airport. Then join the I-5 North for approximately 11.3 miles, leaving at the Harbor Blvd exit. Follow local signs to Disneyland Parking.

Long Beach Airport (LGB):

- There is no Disneyland Resort Express service to this airport.
- The best option is to take a shared shuttle/taxi from the Ground Transportation island. Signs clearly signpost this. Upon exiting baggage claim, cross Donald Douglas Drive to the Ground Transportation island next to the covered parking structure.

Driving:

It is a 13-mile (25-30 min) drive from the airport to Disneyland Resort. Join E Wardlow Road and follow it for 4.2 miles, continue ahead onto Ball Road for 8.3 miles, then turn right onto Disneyland Drive. Follow local signs to Disneyland Parking.

Los Angeles International Airport (LAX):

- **Disneyland Resort Express** – This shuttle service provides direct access to the Disneyland Resort and several local area hotels. After baggage claim, exit the terminal and go to the center island – wait under the sign that says "Flyaway, Buses, Long Distance Vans" for the Disneyland Resort Express – they operate full size coaches only. This service is not run by Disney; it is run by Grayline Anaheim. Hourly departures from 7:50am to 8:00pm. Pick-ups start at Terminal #1. Allow approximately 5 minutes for pick-ups between each terminal. Travel time to the Anaheim Resort Area is approximately 45 minutes, depending on traffic. Fares are $30 each way or $48 round trip for adults. There is often a promotion where children (under 12) go free with fare paying adults. Children are usually priced at $22 each way or $36 round-trip. Visit **www.graylineanaheim.com** for more information.
- **Taxis and shuttle services** – Available from outside each terminal – look for the overhead signs.
- **Public Transport (Metro System)** – After exiting baggage claim, wait in the center islands in front of each terminal under the "LAX Shuttle & Airline Connections" sign. Get the bus/shuttle marked "G" to the Aviation Station. Get the Metro Rail Green Line headed east toward Norwalk. Once you arrive at Norwalk Station, board the Metro Express Line 460 bus headed to the Disneyland Resort. Total journey time is about 1 hour 45 minutes to 2 hours.

Driving:

It is about a 45-minute (33-mile) drive from the airport to the Disneyland Resort. Follow signs for the I-105 East for approximately 16.5 miles, then follow the I-605 South for about 2.5 miles, then CA-91 East for another 7.6 miles, and join the I-5 South for 4.2 miles. Finally, take the exit to Disneyland Drive. Follow the local signs.

Public transportation

From Los Angeles (City Center) to Disneyland

From the LA Union station area to Disneyland Resort by public transportation will take approximately 1 hour 30 minutes to 2 hours depending on transportation connection times. The journey is fairly comfortable but there can be a long wait between buses and trains and it is not something we would recommend doing for a multi-day trip as it would quickly become fatiguing.

From Los Angeles Union Station (Metrolink Station) you will need to get the Orange County Line (about 45 minutes' journey time with several stops) – get off at Anaheim Station. Alternatively, you can get a Pacific Surfliner Amtrak train from LA Union Station to Anaheim Station in about 30 to 45 minutes. Trains are infrequent and are usually every hour but there are often longer gaps between trains.

Once at Anaheim Station you will need to get a bus to the Disneyland Resort. These bus stops are NOT very well signposted and we highly recommend you seek assistance from the train station ticket desk and/or print out a map of the area – especially as bus services are always subject to change. From Anaheim Station, transfer to the Anaheim Resort Transit (ART) Route 15 bus directly to the Disneyland Resort. Alternatively transfer to the OCTA Bus Route 50 and exit at the Katella-Harbor Blvd. stop – from here it is a short walk north along Harbor Blvd. (about 3 blocks) to the Disneyland Resort.

We highly recommend you plan your route using Google Maps' public transportation feature, which allows adequate time for connections and has full and up to date timetables. Alternatively, we find the transport planner on www.metro.net to be very useful as well, giving several different train options. The total cost for the journey is $14 to $20 one way from downtown LA to Disneyland Resort.

Non-Disney hotels to Disneyland Resort

Guests staying on-site at the Disneyland Resort benefit from the proximity of the theme parks to their hotel – it means that they can move from the comfort on their own bed to the comfort of the theme parks within 5 or 10 minutes. For those staying at Non-Disney owned hotels, it is important to consider how far away your hotel is from the Disneyland Resort and how long it will take to reach the theme parks.

Some hotels are within an easy walking distance. Others may have shuttle services available – these are usually complimentary or available for a small fee. If you are using shuttle services make sure to check what time the first and last departures are – they may not be able to get you in early enough for park opening or stay late enough for park closing, so it is important to be aware of this. Also be sure to ask the driver of your shuttle where the return shuttle point is, as drop-off and pick-up locations may vary.

Anaheim Resort Transit (ART)

Many local area hotels do not provide their own shuttle service but are located by Anaheim Resort Transit (ART) bus stops. This is a local bus service that provides service to and from the Disneyland Resort, as well as many other popular locations. There are 19 different routes with all routes stopping at the Disneyland Resort. Most routes have very few stops meaning that transfer times are usually pretty quick. Route 18 will even take you to nearby Knott's Berry Farm theme park from Disneyland.

Buses run every 10 to 30 minutes depending on the season of your visit, and the time of day. They are usually scheduled to begin running well before park opening, and continue after park closing. Buses are fully wheelchair accessible. Tickets from ART can be bought at the Disneyland Bus Loop at a kiosk, or at any hotel located on the route. Tickets must be bought in advance and cannot be bought when boarding.

Tickets are priced at $5, $12 and $20 for 1-day, 3-day and 5-day passes respectively for adults. The pricing for children (Ages 3-9) is $2, $3 and $5 respectively. Children 2 and under travel free and do not need a pass. Learn more at **www.rideart.org**.

Chapter 4

Hotels

The Disneyland Resort offers three on-site resort hotels. These are usually booked as part of packages that include a hotel stay and park tickets combined into one booking.

In our honest opinion, the Disneyland Resort hotels are vastly overpriced, and local alternatives that are just as conveniently located can be found at up to 80% cheaper than these. The quality of the rooms and amenities can vary considerably between hotels, so make sure you do your research.

Having said this, there are several benefits to staying on-site at a Disneyland Resort hotel, including great theming, world-class customer service, staying in the heart of the magic, package delivery to your room and early entry into one of the two theme parks each day.

All rooms at the hotels include a mini-fridge, a safe, coffee making facilities and complimentary Wi-Fi. In multiple-bedroom, villa style accommodation a large refrigerator is available. A swimming pool is also available at all on-site hotels.

Disney's Grand Californian Hotel & Spa:

The highest-class and most expensive hotel at Disneyland Resort, the Grand Californian even has its own private entrance into Disney California Adventure Park. This is a AAA Four-Diamond, award-winning luxury property. The woodland inspired lobby will have you in awe, and is a great place to simply chill out and escape the crowded theme parks – it truly feels like it is a world away.

The lobby even has a roaring fireplace, perfect for snuggling up to in the winter. The hotel is designed in an arts and crafts style of the late 19ᵗʰ and early 20ᵗʰ century, filled with handcrafted details designed to differentiate themselves from the industrial items being produced at the time. There is even a stunning spa (extra charges apply).

There are 948 rooms and 50 Disney Vacation Club villas at this resort.

Rack rates for rooms vary between $379 and $733 per night for a standard room. 1 to 3 bedroom suites are priced at $920 to $1382. All prices exclude tax. Self-parking is charged at $15 per night for up to 2 vehicles, and $22 for valet parking per vehicle.

Top Tip: The hotel offers a free walking tour to both guests and non-guests interested in learning about the building's architectural inspiration. To sign up for this complimentary tour, visit the Guest Services desk at the hotel. The tour is available Sundays, Mondays, Thursdays and Fridays at 1:00pm. Reservations are recommended for the 15 available spots. If space is available, walk-ups are accepted.

Top Tip 2: The rooms available to members of the Disney Vacation Club timeshare scheme offer fantastic views of World of Color.

Dining:
Storyteller's Café – Table Service, character breakfast buffet is $29.99 for adults and $14.99 for children, entrees are $14 to $22 at lunch and $18 to $30 at dinner.
Hearthstone Lounge – Bar and lounge, serves coffees and pastries at breakfast, serves alcoholic and non alcoholic drinks through the rest of the day – snack appetizers are available at $11-$17.
Napa Rose – Table Service, serves dinner only, entrees are $42 to $45
White Water Snacks – Quick Service, breakfast is $5.50-$8, pastries are $2 to $3, lunch and dinner entrees are $7.50 to $11.50

Disney's Paradise Pier Hotel:

This 481-room hotel is themed to reflect the beachside atmosphere of the land with that shares the same name in Disney California Adventure (DCA) park. Annoyingly, the hotel is a 10 to 15-minute walk to the entrance of the theme parks, meaning it is as far as, or further than, many off-site hotels.

In our honest opinion, the hotel is not worth the price paid, but the rooms facing DCA do offer a nice, but by no means perfect, view of World of Color. The walk to DCA is shorter provided you cut through the Grand Californian Hotel located opposite.

Rack rate for standard rooms is $259 to $365 per night. 1 to 2 bedroom suites are priced at $627 to $807 per night. All prices exclude taxes.

Dining:

Disney's PCH Grill – Table Service, character breakfast buffet – adults $31 and children $16, dinner buffet (no characters) is $28 for adults and $14 for children.
Surfside Lounge – Quick Service and bar/lounge, entrees are $6.50-$14, also serves drinks. This lounge serves breakfast.

Disneyland Hotel:

This is the original Disneyland Hotel that has stood on this site since 1955. The hotel was renovated in 2009 to evoke a sense of nostalgia with original Disneyland motifs being spread out throughout the resort, even including monorail themed water slides in the pool area. One of the coolest Disney touches at the hotel is right in your room; every headboard has an outline of Sleeping Beauty Castle. Flick a switch and the headboard will light up with fireworks whilst the song "A Dream is a Wish your Heart Makes" plays.

This AAA Four-Diamond hotel features 969 rooms, including specially themed Disney character suites, and one of the largest convention spaces in the Western United States with 136,000 square feet.

Standard rooms are priced between $329 and $572 per night. 1 to 3 bedroom suites are priced at $677 to $1018 per night. All prices exclude tax.

Dining:
Trader Sam's Enchanted Tiki Bar – Bar and lounge, also serves appetizers at $8.50-$17
Tangaroa Terrace – Quick Service, breakfast entrees are $6.50 to $8, lunch and dinner entrees are $9.50 to $11.50
The Coffee House – Quick Service, sandwiches and salads are $8 to $10, pastries are $3 to $4, also serves hot and cold beverages at $3 to $5.
Goofy's Kitchen – Table service buffet, character dining, does not serve lunch, brunch buffet is $31 for adults and $16 for children, the dinner buffet is $39 for adults and $23 for children
Steakhouse 55 – Table Service, breakfast entrees are $9 to $20, dinner entrees are $31 to $54. This location does not serve lunch.
The Lounge at Steakhouse 55 – Bar and lounge, also serves bar bites, burgers, flatbreads and salads at $10 to $19

Money-saving tips for Disney hotels:

The Disneyland Resort's on-site hotels are definitely pricey for their offering, but that does not mean that deals and discounts are not available. Follow these tips for money-saving advice:

- Visit Disneyland's Special Offers page online at **https://disneyland.disney.go.com/offers-discounts**. At the time of writing offers vary from 20% off hotel rooms to specially priced tickets for those in the military. If you are booking over the phone, make sure to ask what special offers are available (as well as the offer's expiry date); if something comes up that sounds interesting you can always have a think and call back later.

- Choose *when* you stay wisely, as Disney prices its rooms according to how busy they will be. If it knows it can fill all the on-site rooms (such as during Christmas or Spring Break) then room prices will go up, but visit in September when rooms are more likely to be empty and prices are lower. Prices vary significantly across the seasons for the exact same room with the same amenities. You will also find airfares are usually cheaper during the off-season too.

- Discounted stays – Some organizations such as the AAA and AARP often have discounts, which vary depending on the season (note that sometimes there are no discounts at all). These have to be explicitly asked for but are usually in the region of 10-20%, potentially saving you hundreds of dollars.

Non-Disney hotels:

The Disneyland Resort is right in the middle of a bustling town, unlike Walt Disney World Resort in Florida. This means that there is a lot of competition as far as accommodation is concerned. There are off-site hotels, which sometimes are located just a five-minute walk from the theme parks – as close as some of the on-site hotels.

By staying off-site, you will undoubtedly lose some of the Disney magic, but you are also almost *guaranteed* to save a huge amount of money too. You can definitely get more bang for your book as far as facilities are concerned by staying off-site. However, many of the local "hotels" are actually renovated motels; so do bare that in mind when booking.

Personally, from our experience, we do recommend you stay off-site and at a non-Disney hotel as the price markup that Disney demands is not justified. If you want the full package, and money is no object, then of course on-site is the way to go.

With over 100 local area hotels, it is impossible to try them all out for ourselves. So below we have compiled a very helpful table, which includes average user submitted reviews for the hotels as voted by users of Hotels.com.

Prices vary seasonally, and therefore these are merely sample prices. In this example, we are booking stays of 3 nights for two adults and two children staying Tuesday 5th to Friday 8th April 2016. These bookings are being made several months in advance. Prices include all taxes and fees.

This section ranks off-site hotels in three separate grids – based on distance to the Disneyland Resort, average customer review (out of 5) and the hotel's star rating. All hotels in this section are based in Anaheim. Other hotels outside this area are available, but we recommend staying close-by for the full Disney experience.

Non-Disney hotel money-saving tips:

These tips can save you potentially hundreds of dollars on a multi-night stay:

- Check comparison websites – from kayak.com to hotels.com to TripAdvisor's multi hotel search, do not just assume that a hotel price is the same on all booking websites.
- Try the hotel's website directly and compare prices – sometimes the same room is cheaper directly on a hotel's website.
- Coupons – Search online for a coupon, as these can often give you savings of up to 20%. Hotels.com almost always has a 10% off coupon available if you search. Or see hotelcoupons.com who can mail you out a book of coupons (a shipping charge of around $3 applies).
- Mousesavers.com is an incredible resource with a team dedicated solely to saving money at Disney theme parks – any advance, last-minute and coupon-based deals usually make an appearance on here.
- Priceline.com is an interesting concept – you bid for a hotel room in an area, but you are not told the hotel's name. You do, however, get to know the star rating, the general location and the hotel amenities. Within a few hours of placing your bids, and after payment, the name of the hotel is revealed and your card is charged – there are no refunds. With some clever reading of descriptions and looking at the amenities you can usually find out the name of the hotel you are bidding for. Then, simply find the usual going rate and bid lower than that to get a decent discount.

Non-Disney hotels by proximity to Disneyland Park:

Name	Distance to Disneyland (in miles)	Star rating	Average customer review (of 5)	Total price
Anaheim Camelot Inn and Suites	0.43	3	4.1	$564
Carousel Inn and Suites at the Disneyland Resort	0.43	3	3.5	$948
Tropicana Inn and Suites	0.43	2.5	4.0	$628
Anaheim Fairfield Inn by Marriott	0.43	3	4.2	$595
Del Sol Inn – Anaheim Resort	0.45	2	3.6	$590
Anabella Hotel	0.49	3.5	3.6	$632
Best Western Plus Stovall's Inn	0.50	2.5	4.1	$477
Anaheim Plaza Hotel & Suites	0.51	2	3.6	$486
Best Western Plus Pavilions	0.51	2.5	4.0	$400

A guide to walking distances:
- 0.25 miles – 4 minutes
- 0.5 miles – 8 minutes
- 0.75 miles – 12 minutes
- 1 mile – 15 minutes
- 2 miles – 30 minutes

Non-Disney hotels by average customer review:

Name	Average customer review (of 5)	Distance to Disneyland (in miles)	Star rating	Total price
Ayres Hotel Orange	4.6	2.3	2.5	$674
Ayres Hotel Anaheim	4.6	2.6	3	$594
Courtyard Anaheim Theme Park Entrance	4.6	0.4	3	$909
Residence Inn By Marriott Anaheim Resort Area	4.5	1.5	3	$699
DoubleTree Suites by Hilton Anaheim Resort - Conv Centre	4.5	1.0	3.5	$808
Embassy Suites Anaheim - Orange	4.4	2.2	3.5	$437
Residence Inn By Marriott Cypress Orange County	4.4	7.1	3	$772
Hampton Inn Los Angeles/Orange County/Cypress	4.4	5.3	2.5	$593
SpringHill Suites Anaheim Maingate	4.4	0.6	2.5	$746
Hyatt Place at Anaheim Resort/Convention Center	4.4	0.95	3	$730

Non-Disney hotels by Star Rating:

Name	Star rating	Distance to Disneyland (in miles)	Average customer review (of 5)	Total price
Anaheim Marriott Hotel	4	0.78	4.2	$596
Hyatt Regency Orange County	4	1.5	4.3	$630
Embassy Suites Anaheim – Orange	3.5	2.2	4.4	$437
Red Lion Hotel Anaheim	3.5	0.75	3.9	$692
Wyndham Anaheim Garden Grove	3.5	1.6	4.0	$550
Embassy Suites Hotel Anaheim-South	3.5	1.4	4.3	$831
Anaheim Marriott Suites	3.5	1.6	4.3	$767
DoubleTree Suites By Hilton Anaheim Resort – Convention Center	3.5	1.0	4.5	$808
Sheraton Garden Grove – Anaheim South	3.5	1.8	4.2	$445

Note that we do not claim to have vetted all or any of the hotels above, and booking of stays is completely your responsibility. Information provided here is for educational purposes only.

Chapter 5

Tickets

There are many ways to buy entry tickets into the Disneyland Resort - vouchers, annual passes, at the gates, online, at a Disney Store and more. To help you decide, this chapter takes a detailed look at your options. If you have booked a Disneyland on-site hotel package through the Disneyland Resort booking website, or over the phone, then you can skip this section, as your tickets are generally included in your package price.

Buying Tickets at the Park Gates:

If you turn up at the Disneyland Resort spontaneously, you can simply go to the ticket booths by the park entrances and buy your tickets. Yet, as you are reading this guide, this is probably not you. Gate prices are the most expensive and you can get a discount by booking in advance online via ticket brokers, as well as getting special extras for some multi-day tickets.

There are two types of tickets – single park tickets where you can visit one park per day of your ticket's validity; and hopper tickets where you can go between both theme parks during the validity of your ticket.

Gate prices:

- **1 day/1 park** - Adults: $95 to $119; Children $89 to $113
- **1 day/2 parks (hopper)** - Adults: $155 to $169; Children $149 to $164
- **2 days/1 park per day** - Adults: $195; Children $183
- **2 days/2 parks (hopper)** - Adults: $235; Children $223
- **3 days/1 park per day** - Adults: $255; Children $243 – Includes one Magic Morning admission if booked in advance
- **3 days/2 parks (hopper)** - Adults: $295; Children $283 – Includes one Magic Morning admission if booked in advance
- **4 days/1 park per day** - Adults: $280; Children $265 – Includes one Magic Morning admission if booked in advance
- **4 days/2 parks (hopper)** - Adults: $320; Children $305 – Includes one Magic Morning admission if booked in advance
- **5 days/1 park per day** – Adults: $295; Children $280 – Includes one Magic Morning admission if booked in advance
- **5 days/2 parks (hopper)** - Adults: $335; Children $320 – Includes one Magic Morning admission if booked in advance

Ticket prices last increased in February 2016 and usually change once yearly.

Important: As you can see from the pricing grid on the previous page, one-day tickets vary in price. The price varies on the season. There are three seasons: Value, Regular and Peak. The busier the parks are expected to be, the more expensive tickets are. For multi-day tickets, pricing is the same all year.

Note: Children are classed as 3 to 9 year olds; children under 3 enter for free. To buy these tickets, look for the ticket booths just after bag check. Ticket booths start selling tickets one hour before the earliest park's opening time.

Top Tip: Three day or longer Disneyland Resort tickets purchased in advance include one Magic Morning admission that allows you entry one hour before regular park opening into Disneyland Park (with select attractions open) on Tuesday, Thursday or Saturday. Buying these tickets at the theme park gates will not give you this Magic Morning entry.

CityPass:

The 2016 Southern California CityPass is a multi-theme park pass that includes admission to LEGOLAND California, SeaWorld San Diego, and a 3-Day Disneyland Resort Park Hopper Ticket with one Magic Morning admission. Pricing is $341 for ages 10 and up, and $311 for children aged 3 to 9. Children under 3 get free admission to the parks.

If you buy a CityPass at Disneyland Resort, you *will* be entitled to a Magic Morning admission even though it is not an advance purchase.

Online:

You can purchase tickets online at
https://disneyland.disney.go.com/tickets/ - these are the same price as buying at the gates but offer Early Entry options (Magic Mornings) on multi-day tickets. As well as this, buying in advance can save you half an hour or more by not having to wait in line at the ticket booths on your first day.

Top Tip: Tickets can also be bought online on your smartphone at **http://disneyland.com**. No print out is necessary; a unique barcode will be sent to your phone, which you simply show at the turnstiles on the way in. If you are doing this, we recommend you screenshot your ticket on your phone so you can access it even if you do not have Internet access at the turnstiles.

A few more notes:
- Multi-day tickets expire 13 days after the first day of use, or until you have used all your admissions – whichever is sooner.
- Tickets purchased online can be either mailed or printed.

Other ticket brokers are available which offer discounted multi-day tickets such as CheapTickets (**www.cheaptickets.com**) and aRes (**http://arestravel.com**) – both are highly rated online and can offer substantial savings, including free admission days.

Regional Tickets:

- **Australia and New Zealand** – Guests from these two countries can get an exclusive 10-day Disney Vacation Pass, which is a 10-day park hopper ticket with one Magic Morning admission. This ticket is priced at roughly the same price as a 5-day ticket bought on-site. It is only available in Australia and New Zealand. MyPersonalTravelPlanner.com.au seems to be highly-rated seller of these tickets.

- **Canada** – FlightCentre (**www.flightcentre.com**) offers tickets, which are slightly cheaper than those sold directly by Disney. Tickets purchased through BCAA (www.bcaa.com/trip-planning/trip-planning-tools/disneyland-tickets) are the same price as those sold by Disney, or slightly cheaper. In the past these tickets have also entitled you to free parking, saving you $18 per day – do check when buying if this promotion is still valid.

- **United Kingdom** – Use Avios points to book Disneyland Resort tickets. This must be done over the phone – make sure to specify "Disneyland Resort in Anaheim, California" so as to not get Disneyland Paris or Walt Disney World Resort tickets instead. 10,000 Avios points are equal to £50 off tickets. Attraction Tickets Direct is also a trusted provider (www.attraction-tickets-direct.co.uk) that offers discounted tickets, although savings vary according to the exchange rate.

Disney Stores:

You can buy tickets at most Disney Store locations worldwide for the Disneyland Resort. Just ask at the counter. These will be the same price as buying at the ticket booths at the theme parks but will save you time queuing.

Top Tip: If ticket prices are about to go up, you can purchase a physical ticket from the Disney Store and it will still be valid until the expiry date, despite the fact prices have gone up.

California Resident Tickets:

These discounted tickets are available to residents of Southern California in zip codes 90000-93599 and Northern Baja California residents within zip codes 21000-22999. Substantial savings are available. These vary from season to season. In the past savings of up to $70 per ticket have been offered.

Top Ticket Tips:

- Two-park tickets are called "hoppers" as they allow you to hop from park to park during the same day.
- When leaving either park, ask to have your hand stamped to allow re-entry later during the same day.
- You will need at least one day to tour Disney California Adventure Park comfortably and two days to tour Disneyland Park comfortably. More time does mean a more relaxed pace, which you will appreciate whilst on vacation.
- A theme park entry ticket does not get you free parking – that is charged at $18 per day for a standard vehicle.
- If you decide during your stay that you want to extend your ticket length, you can do. However, you must do this before it expires and while your ticket is still valid – this allows you to benefit from much lower rates than buying a second ticket.
- Take a photo of your tickets. Disneyland Resort will replace tickets if they are lost or stolen. However, you will need to know your tickets' barcodes. The best way to know these, of course, is to take a photo of them as soon as you have your tickets in hand. Email these photos to yourself for safe keeping.
- Military discounts are available through base MWR offices. These can also be purchased for friends and family – up to six can be purchased in total. A person with military ID must accompany the group every day. Certain restrictions apply.
- AAA offers its members slightly discounted tickets at some locations.

Annual Passes:

For unlimited admission (up to 365 days per year), an annual pass is your best option. Disney radically overhauled these in October 2015. Your current options are set out below:

There are two annual passes that are available to all guests:

- **Deluxe Passport** – Includes select days of admission to both Disneyland Resort Theme Parks. Parking is not included. Priced at $599. 10% off dining and merchandise. An annual parking pass for the Mickey & Friends parking structure is available for an additional $199.
- **Signature Passport** – Includes select days of admission to both Disneyland Resort theme parks (except peak Holiday period). Includes PhotoPass downloads. 15% off dining and 20% off merchandise. Parking is included. Priced at $849.

- **Signature Plus Passport** – Admission to both Disneyland Resort theme parks every day of the year. Includes PhotoPass downloads. 15% off dining and 20% off merchandise. Parking is included. Priced at $1049.

Local resident annual passes:
Southern California residents can get annual passes at a significant discount.

- **Southern California Annual Passport** – Includes pre-selected days of admission to both Disneyland Resort Theme Parks. Priced at $439. **Note**: Disneyland suspended new sales of this pass in May 2014 – only renewals are currently allowed.

- **Southern California Select Annual Passport** – Includes pre-selected days (weekdays only) of admission to both Disneyland Resort Theme Parks. This pass may still be purchase by local residents only. It is priced at $329. Includes 10% off dining and merchandise.

Blockout dates for annual passes:
The following dates are when your annual pass will not allow you entry into either park until October 2016. The Signature Plus Pass has no blockouts.

	Deluxe Passport	Signature Passport
Dec 2015	19th to 31st	19th to 31st
Jan 2016	1st and 2nd	1st and 2nd
Feb 2016	13th and 14th	None
Mar 2016	19th, 25th and 26th	None
Apr 2016	2nd, 9th, 16th, 23rd and 30th	None
May 2016	7th, 14th, 21st, 28th and 29th	None
Jun 2016	4th, 11th, 18th and 25th	None
July 2016	2nd, 9th, 16th, 23rd and 30th	None
Aug 2016	6th and 13th	None
Sep 2016	3rd	None
Oct 2016	None	None

Annual pass notes:
- So-Cal Select Passport blockout dates are available on the Disneyland Resort locals' website.
- Annual passes are priced the same for both adults and children.
- Local residents can pay for all annual passes, up-front as one amount or opt to pay in installments. Non-residents must pay the full amount at the time of purchase.

Top Tip: If you buy your annual pass on a blockout date you CAN use it for entry that day – this is a good tip to get an extra day out of your pass.

Chapter 6

Disneyland Park

Disneyland Park was the first, and only theme park, that Walt Disney himself ever saw built. It is the theme park that has inspired The Walt Disney Company to bring the magic of Disney parks to other places around the world including Florida, Paris, Hong Kong, Tokyo and this year, Shanghai! Walt wanted a place that the entire family could visit together and enjoy, unlike the dirty amusement parks of the time. Over 60 years later, Disneyland Park is still as magical as it was on opening day.

Note: The approximate attraction wait times listed in this sections are for peak seasons and weekends throughout most of the year.

Main Street, U.S.A.

This is the street you walk down, as you enter the park and see Sleeping Beauty Castle at the end of; it is also where you will walk down to exit at the end of your day. It has shops on both sides of the road - the king of which is the Emporium, where you are sure to find something to buy! There are places to dine along the road too, including Quick Service and Table Service restaurants, as well as snack locations.

City Hall is immediately to your left on Town Square before entering Main Street, U.S.A. itself, this is also known as "Guest Services". Any questions you have can be answered here, they can make dining and tour reservations, help with guest disability cards, and accept complaints and positive comments too.

Top Tip: Celebrating a birthday, graduation, engagement or something else? Pick up a celebration button for free outside City Hall (or at City Hall itself) to let other guests and Cast Members know you are celebrating a special event.

Hidden Secret: If you are particularly keen, you can even become an 'Honorary Citizen of Disneyland Resort' by answering a series of Disney-related questions at City Hall. You'll get a special button to wear!

Attractions:

In addition to the attractions listed on the following pages, you will also find the **Main Street Cinema**, a small cinema area showcasing classic Disney cartoons.

Main Street Vehicles

Fastpass: No
Minimum Height: None
On-ride photo: No
Ride length: 2 to 5 minutes
Average wait times: Less than 5 minutes
Cruise down Main Street, U.S.A. in style by taking one of several vehicles from Town Square to Central Plaza in front of Sleeping Beauty Castle. There are several different kinds of vehicles: a horse-drawn streetcar, a jitney, a fire engine and a bus. Hop on board for some turn of the century fun.

The Disneyland Story: Great Moments with Mr. Lincoln

Fastpass: No
Minimum Height: None
Show length: 15 minutes
Average wait times: Until the next showing starts.
As well as an audio animatronics show, there is also a self-guided tour, which includes a behind-the-scenes look at the making of Disneyland Park including a scale model of the original Disneyland, and rare photos of Walt Disney.

Disneyland Railroad

Fastpass: No
Minimum Height: None
On-ride photo: No
Ride length: 18 minutes for a full loop of the park
Average wait times: Under 10 minutes

Hop aboard the Disneyland Railroad for a circular tour around Disneyland Park on a classic steam locomotive. This is a great relaxing way to get around the park with additional stations in Frontierland, Mickeys' Toontown Fair and Tomorrowland. The full tour takes approximately 18 minutes to complete, with trains usually running every five minutes or so. During off-peak periods you may have to wait significantly longer for a train. The whole tour covers 1.2 miles.

In order to accommodate Disneyland Park's fireworks shows, the Disneyland Railroad will be closed intermittently on evenings with scheduled performances.

Top Tip: Ask to ride in the Lilly Belle car, which only runs at very select times, for a really exclusive journey aboard this railway. There is no charge for this.

Important: As part of the Star Wars Land construction, this attraction (including all stations) is temporarily closed from January 10th, 2016 onwards. A re-opening date has not yet been announced at the time of writing.

Dining:

Market House – Quick Service, sandwiches are $5, pastries and cookies are $2 to $5. This location serves Starbucks beverages.

Carnation Café – Table Service, entrees are $6.50 to $15 at breakfast, entrees are $13 to $18.50 at lunch and dinner.

Gibson Girl Ice Cream Parlor – Snacks, ice creams are $4.50 to $6.

Refreshment Corner – Quick Service, entrees are priced at $7 to $10.50.

Plaza Inn – Character breakfast buffet priced at $30 for adults and $14 for children. Entrees are priced at $12 to $18 at lunch and dinner.

Jolly Holiday Bakery Café – Quick Service, muffins and cookies are $3.50 to $4, desserts are $2 to $6, hot drinks are $2.50 to $5.50, sandwiches, quiches and salads are priced at $8.50 to $11, and soups are about $6.

Other services on Main Street USA:

Many vital guest services are in this entrance area to the park. At the end of Main Street USA (the part closest to the castle) you will find the **Baby Care and Lost Children Center**. Also on this end of the street you will find the **First Aid Center**.

You will also find **Lockers** to store your belongings ($7 to $15 per day) on the right-hand side of Main Street, U.S.A., one building along when walking towards the castle. **Currency Exchange**, **Lost Adults** and **Disneyland Resort Information** can be found inside the City Hall building in the Town Square area.

Although **Lost and Found** is not directly found on Main Street, U.S.A. we thought it would be useful to mention it here – it is found outside the gates of both parks: when facing the Disneyland Park turnstiles walk to the buildings to the left of these turnstiles for Lost and Found.

Adventureland:
Attractions:
Enchanted Tiki Room

Fastpass: No
Minimum Height: None
Show length: 17 minutes
Average wait times: Until the next show starts
Loading: Approximately 230 guests per show
Step into the world of singing flowers and birds in the Enchanted Tiki Room. The original birds created for this attraction were the first ever audio-animatronics! The show's cast features 225 animated singing birds, flowers and tikis. It is perhaps Disneyland's most bewildering attraction and in our opinion is wildly out of date and in need of a replacement. Others would disagree saying it is a Walt Disney original production and should stay to honor its creator.

Tarzan's Treehouse

Walk through Tarzan's tree house in this self-guided and relaxing attraction.

Jungle Cruise

Fastpass: No
Minimum Height: None
On-ride photo: No
Ride length: 7 minutes
Average wait times: 30 to 60 minutes
Loading: 32 people per boat, approximately 1800 guests per hour.
Jump aboard and get ready to set sail through jungles across the world, with a skipper who just can't help but tell the corniest jokes ever. Get ready to hear puns that you never thought anyone would have the guts to perform in public. As boat has its own individual skipper, the ride experience can vary from a hilarious trip, to one where the guide offers minimal enthusiasm.

Fun Fact: The landscape surrounding the Jungle Cruise has evolved into its own ecosystem since opening in 1955. The trees have created a canopy that allows plant species to grow that otherwise would not in Southern California.

Indiana Jones Adventure

Fastpass: Yes
Minimum Height: 46 inches (1.17m)
On-ride photo: No
Ride length: 4 minutes
Average wait times: 45 to 90 minutes
Loading: 12 people per vehicle, approximately 2400 guests per hour
Step into an adventure with Indiana Jones as you journey into the forbidden temple. Board your enhanced motion vehicle and become part of the action – be ready for evil curses, rolling boulders, snakes, bugs, spears and much more on your treacherous journey. A Single Rider line is available for this attraction.

Note: The queue for this ride is relatively fast-moving, but it is very long in terms of distance so be prepared for a bit of a walk. Even in the Fastpass line, from handing in your Fastpass to loading will take 15 to 20 minutes.

Dining:

Tiki Juice Bar – Quick Service, desserts are $3 to $9. Serves the famous Pineapple Dole Whip soft-serve and float.
Tropical Imports – Quick Service, snacks are $2 to $4.50, drinks are $2 to $4.50.
Bengal Barbecue – Quick Service, skewers are $4 to $4.50, sides are $3.50 to $5.50, drinks are $2 to $4.50.

New Orleans Square:
Attractions:
Pirates of the Caribbean

Fastpass: No
Minimum Height: None
On-ride photo: No
Ride length: 15 minutes
Average wait times: 15 to 45 minutes
Loading: About 3400 guests per hour.

On Pirates of the Caribbean, guests board ships which take them on a sixteen-minute journey into a pirate world. There are two small flume drops and the animatronic characters in the attraction are enthralling. Famous songs you will recognize are played throughout the attraction adding to the Pirate-like atmosphere. You will even spot animatronics of Jack Sparrow. This attraction was the last one that Walt Disney himself had a role in designing but has since been updated with modern additions.

The ride loads guests onto the boats efficiently so the queue line is fairly fast moving. Despite its high capacity, because the attraction is so popular it is rare to find an empty queue line here. This is a definite must-see.

Haunted Mansion

Fastpass: No (Yes during the Holiday overlay)
Minimum Height: None
On-ride photo: No
Ride length: 7 minutes
Average wait times: 15 to 45 minutes
Venture through the derelict haunted mansion and ride in "doombuggies" that rotate and tilt to show scenes guests.

There are not any jump-out scares but the loud laughter during the initial walkthrough section may frighten some children, as well as the pop-up ghosts when you reach the cemetery scenes of the ride itself. It is in no way a horror-maze type attraction and you will find that almost everyone loves the ride – it is tongue in cheek ghost humor, but it may frighten younger children.

During the Halloween and Holiday seasons the entire decor is re-done to Tim Burton's 'A Nightmare Before Christmas'. The attraction becomes almost a completely different ride altogether. If you go before or after these seasons, be aware the attraction may be closed for its transition period.

Dining:
Royal Street Veranda – Quick Service, entrees are priced at $10.50, desserts are $4.50 and drinks are $2 to $5.50.
Blue Bayou Restaurant – Table Service, does not serve breakfast, entrees are priced at $27 to $41 at lunch, and $30 to $48 at dinner.
Café Orleans – Table Service, does not serve breakfast, entrees are $16 to $20 at lunch and dinner.
French Market Restaurant – Quick Service, entrees priced at $10 to $14.
Mint Julep Bar (part of French Market Restaurant) – Serves the specialty non-alcoholic Mint Julep drink ($3.60), also serve beignets ($4.50 to $7.50) and other hot and cold drinks ($2 to $4.50).

Frontierland

In addition to the attarctions listed on the following pages, you also want to visit the **Frontierland Shootin' Exposition**, a shooting gallery, at an extra charge. Due to construction work, several of Frontierland's attractions are closed throughout most or all of 2016.

Attractions:
Mark Twain Riverboat

Fastpass: No
Minimum Height: None
On-ride photo: No
Ride length: 12 minutes
Average wait times: Until next boat - boats every 20 minutes.
Loading: Approximately 400 guests per boat.
Sail around Tom Sawyer Island on a leisurely cruise. Note that there is a very, very limited amount of seating and most space is standing room. Closing times vary seasonally but a sign at the loading area will list the day's last trip, as well as the frequency of departures. When 'Fantasmic!' is playing in the evening, the riverboat will close much earlier in the day. This attraction also usually does not commence operation at park opening, but starts later in the morning.

Top Tip: Why not have a go commandeering the riverboat? Make sure to ask a Cast Member if you can visit the wheelhouse before boarding. If possible, you will be allowed to ring the riverboat bell, steer the riverboat and be given a certificate at the end.

Important: As part of the Star Wars Land construction, this attraction temporarily closed in January 2016. A re-opening date has not yet been announced at the time of writing.

Pirate's Lair on Tom Sawyer Island

Fastpass: No
Minimum Height: None
Walkthrough length: As long as you like. About 30 minutes to see it all.
Average wait times: Under 5 minutes
Loading: By raft – about 20 to 30 guests per raft
Take a raft over to Tom Sawyer's Island and explore this well-themed area with pirate nods.

Important: As part of the Star Wars Land construction, this attraction temporarily closed in January 2016. A re-opening date has not yet been announced at the time of writing.

Sailing Ship Columbia

Fastpass: No
Minimum Height: None
On-ride photo: No
Ride length: 12 minutes
Average wait times: Until next boat – boats every 20 minutes.
Loading: Approximately 300 guests per ride.
Sail around Tom Sawyer Island on the Sailing Ship Columbia. Note that there is a very, very limited amount of seating and most space is standing room. Closing times vary seasonally but a sign at the loading area will list the day's last trip, as well as the frequency of departures – when Fantasmic is playing in the evenings the Sailing Ship Columbia will close much earlier. You may find that during non-peak seasons this attraction does not operate. When it is open, it usually does not commence operation at park opening, but starts later in the morning.

Important: As part of the Star Wars Land construction, this attraction temporarily closed in January 2016. A re-opening date has not yet been announced at the time of writing.

Big Thunder Mountain Railroad

Fastpass: Yes
Minimum Height: 40 inches (1.02m)
On-ride photo: No
Ride length: 3 minutes 30 seconds
Average wait times: 60 to 90 minutes
Loading: 30 passengers per train, rows of two
Jump aboard a family rollercoaster sure to bring a smile to everyone's face. This ride lasts about 3 and a half minutes, which is unusually lengthy for a rollercoaster.

You will see explosives, western towns, flooding caves, bats and more on this wild, wild ride! This is a great family ride and a way to get kids into rollercoasters, being the first real rollercoaster for many.

Having just gone through a major refurbishment in 2014, the ride is smoother than ever and has some incredible new special effects.

Dining:
River Belle Terrace – Quick Service, entrees are $7.50 to $9 at breakfast, $11 to $12 at lunch. Offers a Fantasmic dining package.
Stage Door Café – Quick Service, does not serve breakfast, entrees are $8 to $10.
The Golden Horseshoe – Quick Service, does not serve breakfast, entrees are $9.50 to $10.
Rancho del Zocalo Restaurante – Quick Service, does not serve breakfast, entrees are $10.50 to $14.

Critter Country
Attractions:
Davy Crockett's Explorer Canoes

Fastpass: No
Minimum Height: None
On-ride photo: No
Ride length: Approximately 20 minutes
Average wait times: Under 20 minutes
Loading: Up to 20 guests per canoe, plus two Cast Members
This is yet another way to get around Tom Sawyer Island. This time, *you* provide the power as you use a real canoe to sail around the island. With twenty of you powering at the same time, it is less effort than it might appear – an interesting and unique theme park experience. This attraction does not operate during non-peak days.

Important: As part of the Star Wars Land construction, this attraction temporarily closed in January 2016. A re-opening date has not yet been announced at the time of writing.

The Many Adventures of Winnie the Pooh
Fastpass: No
Minimum Height: None
On-ride photo: No
Ride length: 2 minutes 45 seconds
Average wait times: Under 15 minutes. Almost always a walk-on.
Loading: 6 to 9 guests per honeypot.
Hop inside one of Pooh's honey pots and explore his many adventures.

This is a slow, gentle ride through the stories of Winnie the Pooh. The ride itself is filled with bright colors that should excite the little ones.

Even on busy days, this ride regularly has a wait time of less than 15 minutes. This version of the ride is slightly superior to the one at Walt Disney World Resort, yet it is so hidden at Disneyland Park that lines are usually short or non-existent.

Splash Mountain

Fastpass: Yes
Minimum Height: 40 inches (1.02m)
On-ride photo: Yes
Ride length: 10 minutes
Average wait times: 30 to 70 minutes
Loading: 6 people per log, about 1500 guests per hour.
Hop on a ride inspired by Br'er Rabbit's adventure and the 'Song of the South' film. This is a log flume-style ride with a long indoor portion, vaguely following the story of the movie. Enjoy the great music, the animatronics and the details, small indoor drops, as well as the big 52-foot drop at the end. You can get soaked on this ride – unlike its Walt Disney World counterpart, which merely sprays its guests. A single rider line is available.

Dining:

Harbour Galley – Quick Service, does not serve breakfast, entrees are $9.50 to $15.
Hungry Bear Restaurant – Quick Service, does not serve breakfast, entrees are $9.50 to $11.

Fantasyland:

During nights when fireworks are performed, parts of this land close early. Consult a Cast Member or your park times guide for specific information. If the park is open for a while after the fireworks, these Fantasyland attractions will re-open until park closing time.

Attractions:

Fantasyland is filled with attractions which are mainly targeted at the younger members of the family.

Sleeping Beauty Castle Walkthrough

Step inside Sleeping Beauty Castle itself and see scenes that retell the story of the Disney classic 'Sleeping Beauty'. This is a self-guided tour and will take between five and ten minutes to see it all. The entrance can be difficult to find: when looking at the back of the castle, it is to the right – you go up a staircase into the main castle area.

Alice in Wonderland

Fastpass: No
Minimum Height: None
On-ride photo: No
Ride length: 3 minutes
Average wait times: 15 to 30 minutes
Loading: 4 guests per vehicle, two rows of two people.
This is the only Alice in Wonderland themed dark ride in the world and we think it is the most elaborate attractions in Fantasyland– with seemingly endless scenes. You are invited to celebrate your "unbirthday" with Alice and the Mad Hatter – and you get to meet their friends along the way. Due to having an outdoor section, this attraction does not operate in inclement weather and until outdoor surfaces are dry.

The attraction went through a major refurbishment in 2014 and now has new projection effects that add to the storytelling experience.

Bibbidi Bobbidi Boutique

Behind the castle, you will find the **Bibbidi Bobbidi Boutique**, a makeover salon, where little girls can be transformed into princesses complete with make-up, a Disney costume dress and a hair do. Packages for this experience vary between $60 to $195 plus tax depending on what you choose to have done.

Boys do not have to miss out though and can take part by purchasing the rather reasonably priced "Knight Package" for $20 plus tax that includes hairstyling with gel, confetti and a sword and shield to keep.

Reservations can be made up to 60 days in advance and are strongly recommended. To book your appointment with a Fairy Godmother-in-training, you can call 714-781-STYLE or 714-781-7895.

Snow White's Scary Adventures
Fastpass: No
Minimum Height: None
On-ride photo: No
Ride length: 2 minutes
Average wait times: 15 to 30 minutes
Loading: 4 people per car, 2 rows of two people
Step inside the world of Snow White as you venture through the major scenes in the movie on a classic dark ride. Although the ride is for the most part tame, there are some moments that may frighten younger children – these make up a significant portion of the ride.

Peter Pan's Flight

Fastpass: No
Minimum Height: None
On-ride photo: No
Ride length: 3 minutes
Average wait times: 30 to 45 minutes
Loading: 2 to 3 people per ship

Board a flying pirate ship and take a voyage through the world of Peter Pan and Never Never Land. The scenes will be both besides you and (because you are in a flying pirate ship) below you too! The interior to this ride is stunning from the moment you step in and the whole experience is truly immersive. The low capacity of the ride coupled with the immense popularity of the characters causes long queues to form which do not dissipate throughout the day. This is one of Disneyland's most popular rides but it does not offer Fastpass.

If you are afraid of heights, this ride may not be suitable for you as the ships give the sensation of flight and at times you will be several feet off the ground.

This ride has been 'plussed' for the 60th anniversary and now includes special projection effects that add detail to this great classic attraction.

Pinocchio's Daring Journey

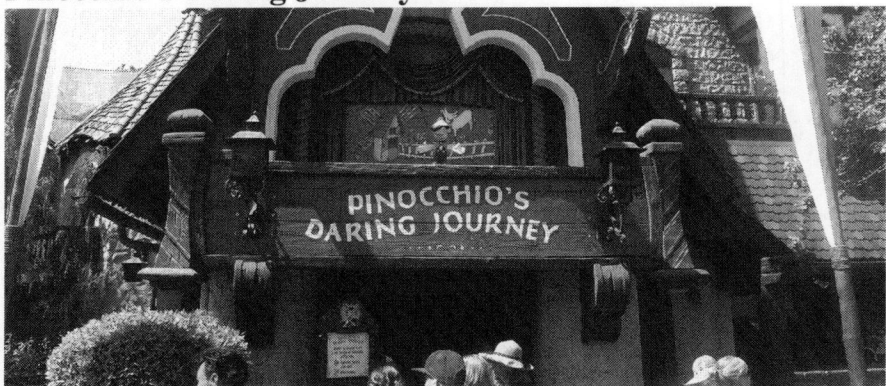

Fastpass: No
Minimum Height: None
On-ride photo: No
Ride length: 3 minutes
Average wait times: 15 to 30 minutes
Loading: 4 people per car, two per row
Ride through the story of Pinocchio and see the tales from the book come to life in front of your very eyes. There are a few clever effects inside the ride and, as with the film, there are also some darker moments that may frighten younger children, though these do pass by relatively quickly and are generally fine for most children.

This ride is not a major attraction like *Peter Pan's Flight*, but it still gets long queues due to the popularity of the character, and the limited ride capacity.

Mr. Toad's Wild Ride
Fastpass: No
Minimum Height: None
On-ride photo: No
Ride length: 2 minutes
Average wait times: 20 to 30 minutes
Loading: 4 people per car, two per row
Another dark ride in the same vain as *Snow White* and *Pinocchio*, but this time it is the story of Mr. Toad that you will be making your way through. Of the three similar dark rides (the others being *Pinocchio* and *Snow White*), this is the one with the slowest moving line and is generally the most popular.

King Arthur Carrousel

Fastpass: No
Minimum Height: None
On-ride photo: No
Ride length: 1 minute 30 seconds
Average wait times: 5 to 10 minutes
Loading: Up to 1 adult and 1 child per horse, about 100 guests per ride
This is a beautiful vintage carrousel that is sure to create memories to guests of all ages. This truly is a ride for every member of the family. It is a popular ride but does not get huge queue lines – wait times do not usually exceed 20 minutes.

Located in front of the carrousel is the Sword in the Stone. Try pulling it out, and if you are the right person for the job and you get the sword out, you might just be crowned King or Queen of the kingdom!

Dumbo The Flying Elephant

Fastpass: No
Minimum Height: None
On-ride photo: No
Ride length: 1 minute 30 seconds
Average wait times: 30 to 45 minutes
Loading: 1 to 3 people per Dumbo
Step aboard and fly through the skies with Dumbo! This is one of the most popular rides in the whole of the Disneyland Resort across both theme parks. Situated right in the center of Fantasyland, it offers great views of the surrounding area, as well being a whole lot of fun. In front of the seats of each Dumbo elephant there is a lever which allows you to lift your Dumbo up or down into the air!

Due to its popularity amongst both children and adults alike, its slow loading nature and low hourly capacity, *Dumbo* has reasonably long queues all day long - try to ride it during parades, extended park hours, or the beginning or end of the day for the shortest waits.

Casey Jr. Circus Train

Fastpass: No
Minimum Height: None
On-ride photo: No
Ride length: 3 minutes 30 seconds
Average wait times: Under 20 minutes
Based on the character from Dumbo, Casey Junior is a little circus train that will take you on a ride around scenes from many classic Disney films. This is a great family ride for those with little ones! Note that adults will be cramped on this ride - and two adults next to each other will have to squeeze in very tightly!

You will whizz by castles and other story pieces retelling some of Disney's classic tales. For a more leisurely view of these scenes, try the Storybook Land Canal Boats attraction located next to this ride.

Top Tip: If you want a specific seat, ask the Cast Members and they can accommodate your request. You can ride at the front by the engine, in a cage or in an open air carriage.

Storybook Land Canal Boats

Fastpass: No
Minimum Height: None
On-ride photo: No
Ride length: 6 minutes
Average wait times: 25 to 45 minutes
Loading: Up to 15 guests per boat

This is a relaxing ride on a boat past models of classic childhood tales. It is a nice, serene change from some of the busier attractions in the park, and you will have a Cast Member on your boat telling you about the models you can see. Wait times are consistently in the 25 to 45 minutes range right from park opening until closing time. If you want to do this ride with short waits, you will want to head here first thing in the morning.

Mad Tea Party

Fastpass: No
Minimum Height: None
On-ride photo: No
Ride length: 1 minute 30 seconds

Average wait times: Less than 20 minutes
Loading: 3 to 4 guests per teacup, 18 teacups – about 1100 riders per hour
Hop inside one of the teacups from Alice in Wonderland and start spinning wildly. The ride functions much like any other teacup ride around the world, where you have a wheel at the center of the cup and you can turn it to spin yourself round faster, or leave it alone and have a more relaxing spin. This attraction does not operate in the rain, or immediately after raining.

Matterhorn Bobsleds

Fastpass: No
Minimum Height: 42 inches (1.07m)
On-ride photo: No
Ride length: 2 minutes
Average wait times: 20 to 30 minutes
Loading: Single-file seating for up to six people, over 1500 riders per hour.
Step onto the world's first steel rollercoaster at the Matterhorn Bobsleds. The ride is actually composed of two different rides on separate tracks. You climb up to the top of the mountain in your bobsled, when suddenly you encounter the yeti and from there it is a race down the mountain until you reach the splashdown. This attraction's animatronics and special effects were upgraded for the 60th anniversary and the yeti looks more realistic than ever!
Note: This is quite a rough coaster due to its age and we think is really quite uncomfortable from start to finish.

Top Tip 1: A Single Rider line is available –ask the Cast Member at the main attraction entrance by the undercover queue area to use it.
Top Tip 2: If both sides of the attraction are operating, the side closest to Fantasyland usually has a shorter queue.

it's a small world

Fastpass: No
Minimum Height: None
On-ride photo: No
Ride length: 14 minutes
Average wait times: 15 to 30 minutes
Loading: 4 or 5 people per row, 4 rows per boat

One of the most memorable, and popular park attractions, "it's a small world" features hundreds of dolls singing along to a catchy tune about the uniting of the world. As your boat sails leisurely through the attraction you can enjoy sights and sounds from around the world.

The loading system is efficient, meaning that the number of people who can enjoy the ride every hour is high. This means that wait times are usually relatively low and there is a constantly moving queue line. This is a great Disney classic that, although not based on any film franchise, is a "must-do" for most visitors.

Top Tip: Look out for the dolls designed to look like Disney characters on the ride. You will see everyone from Stitch to Woody.

Dining:

Village Haus Restaurant – Quick Service, does not serve breakfast, entrees are priced at $8 to $11.50.
Edelweiss Snacks – Serves turkey legs, corn on the cob, and drinks. Chimichangas are priced at $6.30 and turkey legs are priced at $10.50.
Troubadour Tavern – Snacks are priced at $4 to $7, and Bratwurst Sausages are priced at $8.50.

Fantasyland Entertainment: Fantasy Faire

Opened in 2013, Fantasy Faire is the latest extension of Fantasyland and consists of several sections. At the Royal Plaza you will find princess meet and greets, usually with three princesses available at a time, and at the Royal Theatre you can see live shows throughout the day. This area is also filled with great photo opportunities everywhere – from the amazing animatronic Figaro to Rapunzel's tower.

Mickey and the Magical Map at Fantasyland Theatre

Show length: 20 minutes
This show is a definite must do – combining advanced screen technology with singing and dancing. Plus, with all of your favorite characters in one place, you definitely can't miss this show. You can expect some amazing singing, as well as some heartwarming moments too. Try and get a seat as close to the center as possible for the best view.

Mickey's Toontown Fair

Come and see where Mickey and his cartoon pals live. Toontown closes early on nights when Disneyland Park presents a fireworks spectacular.

Attractions:

As well as the following attractions in Mickey's Toontown Fair, you may also want to visit **Chip 'n Dale Treehouse** (a rope and ladders course) and **Donald's Boat** (a water play area).

Roger Rabbit's Car Toon Spin

Fastpass: Yes
Minimum Height: None
On-ride photo: No
Ride length: 3 minutes 30 seconds
Average wait times: 30 to 60 minutes
Loading: 2 guests per car.
Step into the world of Roger Rabbit in this dark ride with a twist!
On this ride you can either choose to simply sit back and enjoy the storyline or choose to turn the wheel in the center of your taxi to spin round as you go through the ride – it is a surprisingly surreal experience to have this level of control on a dark ride and makes every ride different from the last.

Gadget's Go Coaster

Fastpass: No
Minimum Height: 35 inches (0.89m)
On-ride photo: No
Ride length: 1 minute
Average wait times: 20 to 45 minutes
Loading: 2 adults per car, 16 guests per train
A small rollercoaster for kids with one drop and a few turns – the ride is rather underwhelming, especially given the typically long wait times. The ride time is actually less than a minute and even if there is no queue you will probably feel underwhelmed. It is a good starter coaster for kids though, before getting them on the likes of Big Thunder Mountain Railroad.

There are also a variety of permanent **meet and greet opportunities** in this land of the park, including:

- Goofy's Playhouse
- Mickey's House and Meet Mickey
- Minnie's House

Dining:
Pluto's Dog House – Quick Service, does not serve breakfast, a hot dog with chips or apple slices is priced at $6.80.
Daisy's Diner – Quick Service, does not serve breakfast, pizzas are priced at $8.
Clarabelle's Frozen Yogurt – Quick Service, does not serve breakfast, salads and sandwiches are priced at $7 to $10.

Tomorrowland
Attractions:
In addition to the attractions that follow, you may also want to visit **Starcade**, an arcade with extra charges.

The Tomorrowland area hosts the **Season of the Force** celebration from November 2015 onwards. As of April 2016 the season is still running with no end date announced at the moment for this celebration. During this time Space Mountain has a re-themed interior and is called Hyperspace Mountain, Star Wars Launch Bay opens (more details later), Star Tours has a new scene added, Captain EO is replaced by a Star Wars tribute, and the Jedi Training Academy has been reimagined with new characters.

Astro Orbiter

Fastpass: No
Minimum Height: None
On-ride photo: No
Ride length: 1 minute 30 seconds
Average wait times: 20 to 30 minutes
Loading: 1 or 2 guests per rocket ship
Soar above Tomorrowland in your very own rocket. This is a spinning-type ride similar to *Dumbo* in Fantasyland. However, on this ride guests can go much higher and tilt both inwards and outwards depending on their height. At the top you really gather some speed. It is a lot of fun but we would not say it is a must-do, because of the similarity to other attractions such as *Dumbo*. Fitting two adults into one of these rockets can be quite a challenge so we would recommend asking for one rocket per adult – a rocket can usually be shared by an adult and a child.

Star Tours – The Adventures Continue

Fastpass: Yes
Minimum Height: 40 inches (1.02m)
On-ride photo: No
Ride length: 4 minutes 30 seconds
Average wait times: 30 to 45 minutes

From the moment you step into the queue line you are transported into an intergalactic spaceport with adverts for various destinations and overhead announcements of flights leaving. As you travel through the Space terminal you will see StarSpeeders, an alien air traffic control station, R2-D2, C3PO, and many robots hard at work to make your journey into space unforgettable.

Staff will split you into groups and then you board your vehicle for your tour to one of many planets. Each ride is an unforgettable adventure and each time you experience the ride it should be slightly different, with over 50 different combinations of scenes picked randomly! A new scene was even added in November 2015 before the launch of the new Star Wars movie.

However, if you are prone to motion sickness or are not comfortable with confined spaces, *Star Tours* will most probably not be for you. If you want a milder ride, ask to be sat at the front row as this is actually the middle of the vehicle and therefore means fewer sudden movements.

Buzz Lightyear Astro Blasters

Fastpass: No
Minimum Height: None
On-ride photo: No
Ride length: 5 minutes
Average wait times: 25 to 45 minutes
Loading: 2 guests per vehicle

This ride is great family-fun as you step aboard the Space Cruisers and use the onboard laser guns to shoot at targets around you – you will be helping out Buzz Lightyear, and racking up points as you shoot the different targets. Different targets are worth different amounts of points and there are even hidden targets that allow you score thousands of points in one go.

You can even affect the direction of your Space Cruiser with a joystick in the middle and turn the car the other way if you spot a target your friend has not.

If you have been to Walt Disney World this is similar to the ride in Magic Kingdom Park but with different scenes and with detachable guns for even more fun!

At the end of the ride, the person with the most points wins. It is competitive and endlessly re-rideable. Great fun!

Top Tip: After the ride, you can email your on-ride photo to yourself for free at the self-service machines. It is the only attraction at the resort to allow you to do this. Neat!

Finding Nemo Submarine Voyage

Fastpass: No
Minimum Height: None
On-ride photo: No
Ride length: 15 minutes
Average wait times: 30 to 75 minutes
Loading: 40 seats per submarine

Journey into the oceans in search of Nemo and his friends in this attraction that is unique to Disneyland Park. Once you board the submarines, experience what it is like to go underwater through the use of special effects. Once underwater you can look out of portholes into the big blue. This attraction is great family fun though the interior may be claustrophobic for some – it really does feel like you are in a genuine submarine. This is a must-do in our opinion!

Top Tip: Due to its low capacity, lack of Fastpass and extreme popularity, we recommend you make this attraction the first visit of your day if you want to experience it with minimum waits. Alternatively, visit it at the end of your day just before the park closes. Wait times do not really dip throughout the day, as this is a very popular ride.

Disneyland Monorail

Fastpass: No
Minimum Height: None
On-ride photo: No
Ride length: 15 minutes for a round trip, 6 minutes for a one-way trip.
Average wait times: Usually under 20 minutes. There are longer waits first thing in the morning and in the evening.

Unlike the monorails at some other Disney resorts, this ride actually travels both in and out of the theme parks. You will begin right in the heart of Tomorrowland, go through Disney California Adventure's backstage areas and the grounds of the Grand Californian Hotel, and then over to Downtown Disney. Guests may board at either Downtown Disney (Valid theme park admission is required) or in Tomorrowland. All guests must exit at Tomorrowland station – whether they have completed a full loop or not.

Star Wars Launch Bay

Step inside and celebrate all things Star Wars. Inside guests can experience special character encounters with Darth Vader and Chewbacca; watch exclusive interviews with key members who have produced the Star Wars films at the Launch Bay Theater; explore The Cantina; play video games at the Game Center; explore galleries with props and décor from the movies; and purchase merchandise at the Cargo area.

Autopia

Fastpass: Yes
Minimum Height: 32 inches (0.82m) to ride with another rider who is 54 inches (1.37m) or taller. Guests must be at least 54 inches (1.37m) to ride alone.
On-ride photo: No
Ride length: 5 minutes
Average wait times: 30 to 60 minutes
Loading: 1 adult, or 1 adult and 1 child per car
Hop aboard one of the Autopia cars and take it for a spin. This is undoubtedly one of the most popular rides with kids, particularly with little boys who get to drive a car for the very first time – and you even get given your own Tomorrowland driving license in the queue line as a memento.

The cars are guided on rails so you can't really go too far wrong, but you have full control over the speed and you can even race others. The ride is open to people of all ages (subject to height restrictions) and is definitely worth a visit – it is good family fun. This ride gets long queues due to its popularity and low capacity. Use Fastpass to save yourself a lot of time.

Space Mountain

Fastpass: Yes
Minimum Height: 40 inches (1.02m)
On-ride photo: Yes
Ride length: 3 minutes
Average wait times: 45 to 90 minutes
Loading: 12 passengers per rocket
Space Mountain is a rollercoaster through space designed with the family in mind - it has no loops or inversions and recreates the feeling of soaring through the galactic world. We strongly recommend a Fastpass as the queue line is not themed at all and ends up feeling even longer than it really is. Alternatively, get to this ride first or last to minimize wait times. Note that this ride is less exciting and tamer than its Walt Disney World counterpart, and much tamer than the Disneyland Paris version.

Note: During the Star Wars-themed 'Season of the Force' special event, this attraction is transformed into 'Hyperspace Mountain' with a rethemed interior. Also, during Halloween, the interior is re-themed to 'Space Mountain: Ghost Galaxy'.

Tomorrowland Theater – Captain EO
Fastpass: No
Minimum Height: None
Show length: 17 minutes
Average wait times: Until next show. Shows every 20 minutes
Fans of Michael Jackson fans cannot miss this show! Disney does its theatre shows in a completely different manner to all other theme parks and Captain EO is no exception - a 3D film with some extra in-theatre special effects, makes this a nostalgic blast from the past.

Starring Michael Jackson himself, two original songs, a heartwarming storyline and an astounding cast, the characters transform themselves into part of Jackson's band to fight the forces of evil with music! Admittedly, the storyline is a little limp and the effects are old-fashioned, however it is still a fun bit of nostalgia.

Fun fact: The film is 17 minutes in length and cost over $30million to make, making it the most expensive film per minute at the time is was created.

Important: Since July 2014, this theatre has been used to show film previews at times, and at other times it has shown Captain EO. At the time of writing, the theater, as part of the season of the force, is showing "Star Wars: Paths of the Jedi" – a 10-minute retelling of the blockbuster *Star Wars* saga and get a peek at the future of the galaxy. It is unclear what the theater will be used for throughout 2016.

Dining:

Galactic Grill – Quick Service, entrees are priced at $6.50 to $9 at breakfast, and $9 to $11.50 at lunch and dinner. Specialty Star Wars-themed items may be available.

Redd Rockett's Pizza Port – Quick Service, does not serve breakfast, entrees are $7 to $11, whole pizzas are priced at $35 to $40.

Disneyland Park Entertainment:

Disneyland Park is filled with all kinds of entertainment. It offers more than enough entertainment experiences to fill an entire day, without even going on any of the rides. From parades to live shows to character meets, there is a huge variety of things to experience. The entertainment really is what makes Disneyland Park what it is today; it is as much of an experience as the rides, so make sure you do not miss out.

Character Appearances:

Disney characters have both regularly scheduled meet and greets that are announced in advance on the times guide, and random meet and greets. This is a general guide, but of course you may see any character, anywhere throughout your trip. That is part of the fun of visiting Disneyland!

You will find the princesses in the Fantasy Faire area of Fantasyland. Merida meets in Fantasyland by "it's a small world" – a very popular meet and greet. Aladdin and Jasmine can sometimes be found in Aladdin's Oasis in Adventureland, though this meeting location is used infrequently.

Tinker Bell and other fairies can be met at Pixie Hollow located to the right of the castle. Princess Tiana and Prince Naveen can usually be met in the New Orleans Square area. At Mickey's Toontown Fair you can see Mickey, Minnie, Pluto, Goofy and other pals.

On Main Street, Town Square and in Fantasyland you will often see random characters. Winnie the Pooh, Tigger and friends meet by the Winnie the Pooh ride in Critter Country.

Live music:

In Tomorrowland during peak season you can sometimes hear rock groups playing on the stage where the Jedi Training usually takes place. This will be on the park's times guide if it is taking place. Outside Refreshment Corner you can hear the piano player who plays songs at your request. Near the waterfront in the New Orleans area of the park you might find the Bootstrappers performing live music. Plus, on Main Street do not miss the Dapper Dans, a barbershop quartet, who usually perform at regular intervals in the mornings and early afternoons.

Jedi Training – Trials of the Temple:

Located on the Tomorrowland Terrace Stage, this show allows young Padawans aged 4 to 12 to learn to use a lightsaber and battle a Star Wars villain. You can either sit back and watch the show or become part of it!

Golden Horseshoe – Laughing Stock Co.:
This comedy show performs inside the Golden Horseshoe Saloon and
sometimes outside too. Each show is unique and improvised depending on
the crowd. This is a really fun show that is not to be missed.

Flag Retreat Ceremony:
In the USA, it is customary that all stars and stripes flags be lit up at
nighttime, or brought down at dusk. This ceremony occurs at around dusk
where a guard lowers the flag and folds it up while the Disneyland marching
band plays patriotic songs. Members of the armed forces are encouraged to
participate. For reference the "flags" on top of buildings on Main Street,
U.S.A. are not real flags (with either extra stripes or stars missing) and
therefore are not lit up.

Nighttime Shows:

For the 60th anniversary celebrations, which continue through September 2016, the Disneyland Resort has a roster of new nighttime entertainment.

Fireworks:

Disneyland has a fireworks show above the castle throughout the year on most nights – shows change seasonally varying from "Remember... Dreams Come True", and "Magical" featuring Tinker Bell, to the July 4th, Halloween, Holiday and New Year firework displays. Whatever the season, there is something to light up the sky and create a finale to your night. The nighttime fireworks usually last between 12 and 14 minutes, depending on the show.

Note that fireworks at Disneyland Park are shown daily during peak periods, and on select nights during off-peak periods.

During the 60th anniversary celebrations, a new nighttime spectacular called "Disneyland Forever" lights up the sky. For the first time, as well as the fireworks, there are projections up and down Main Street USA's buildings, on the castle itself and around Disneyland Park. There are even other touches from the roofs of Main Street throughout the show. Exceptionally, "Disneyland Forever" will be performed every evening throughout the 60th anniversary celebrations. On very peak dates, the fireworks will be performed twice nightly.

The best place to watch the show is around Central Plaza in front of Sleeping Beauty Castle, but unfortunately there is not enough space here for all guests. Fireworks can be viewed from many locations around the parks so just make sure you are in a position where you can see the castle without anything blocking your view and you are bound to enjoy it.

Some parts of Fantasyland close well before the fireworks begin and re-open when the fallout has been cleared (which is usually about 15 to 20 minutes after they end), if the park remains open after the fireworks. Signs will be positioned throughout Fantasyland and Cast Members will be able to provide you with more detailed information on these times.

Attractions that will be off-limits during this time are Alice in Wonderland, Mr. Toad's Wild Ride, Snow White's Scary Adventure's, Pinocchio, King Arthur's Carousel, Dumbo the Flying Elephant and Sleeping Beauty Castle walkthrough. If you time this right, you can get on a ride straight after the fireworks with little to no wait. Toontown will close before the fireworks and will not reopen after them.

Fantasmic:

Important: As part of the Star Wars Land construction, Fantasmic has temporarily been on hiatus since January 2016 onwards. A re-opening date has not yet been announced at the time of writing.

Fantasmic is a true nighttime spectacular. Expect appearances from your favorite classic Disney characters on stage, an animatronic dragon, pyrotechnics, water fountains, fireworks and an enthralling story with Mickey in his Sorcerer Apprentice attire. Unlike the Walt Disney World version, which takes place in an amphitheater, here the show happens on Tom Sawyer Island and the Rivers of America in the heart of Frontierland.

Fantasmic is not performed every night of the year, and usually is only shown when the park is open past 10:00pm. Be sure to consult the official Disneyland website before arrival or when booking to avoid disappointment. During peak periods of the year, there can be up to two shows per night.

If you have purchased 'Glow with the Show' light-year Mickey ears bring them along, as they will play a part in this show.

Reserve your place for the show:
In order to watch Fantasmic, you should watch from one of the designated viewing areas. To stand in these specific viewing areas will require a Fastpass ticket reservation much like "World of Color" at Disney California Adventure park (more on this later in the guide). Chairs are not provided in any of the viewing areas.

Beginning at Disneyland Park opening, "Fantasmic!" Fastpass distribution takes place along Big Thunder Trail in Frontierland. These are distributed on a first-come, first-served basis until one hour prior to show time or while supplies last, whichever comes first. Each "Fantasmic!" Fastpass will indicate the assigned show time, suggested return time and assigned viewing section.

A non-ticketed area is also available in the "Fantasmic!" viewing area each night for limited stand-by viewing on a first-come, first-served basis. Once all tickets for the first show have been distributed, Fastpass distribution for the second show will begin if two shows are scheduled for one night. Similar to the "World of Color" Fastpass, the "Fantasmic!" Fastpass does not affect your ability to obtain Fastpass for other attractions.

Guests also have the option to receive a "Fantasmic!" Fastpass with the purchase of "Fantasmic!" dining packages, including dinner at Blue Bayou Restaurant (from 4:00pm - $61 per adult, $23 per child), special table-service seating at River Belle Terrace (from 3:00pm - $42 per adult, $22 per child), a dessert party at Hungry Bear Restaurant ($30 per person, tax included), on-the-go options (from Aladdin's Oasis - $20 per adult, $14 per child) and more. For reservations, go online or call (714) 781-DINE or (714) 781-3463.

River-front viewing is available for all three options (dining packages, FASTPASS and stand-by), however a portion of the centrally located sections is reserved for guests with Blue Bayou Restaurant and River Belle Terrace dining packages.

Guests are of course welcome to watch the show from non-approved viewing areas but these are unlikely to be great viewing spots. This new system should avoid people having to stake out spots hours in advance but you will still want to turn up early to get the best spot in your section for optimal viewing.

Top Tip: When the show is on twice a night, the second performance will be much less busy so you will have more of a chance of getting a good spot.

Parades:
Mickey's Soundsational Parade

Soundsational is our favorite daytime parade from all the Disney parks worldwide. This 15-minute parade offers a catchy soundtrack, live music, creative floats and a lot of characters on foot dancing around. The parade debuted in 2011.

The parade features floats and music from Aladdin, The Little Mermaid, the Three Caballeros, Princess and the Frog, Peter Pan and Mary Poppins to just name a few. The theme of the parade is a musical extravaganza, with live instruments played along the route by performers, as well as the soundtrack played via the park speakers.

The parade route starts at the right hand side of Town Square, goes around Town Square itself, up Main Street, U.S.A., to the right of the castle hub, towards and past the Matterhorn, and finally towards the right of "it's a small world" in Fantasyland. This route is marked on your park map. If the parade is being shown twice in the same day, the parade route may be reversed for one of these performances.

Main Street, U.S.A. is generally the most crowded area to watch the parade from, so if you want a spot here, stake it out early. Some of the best viewpoints on the route are by "it's a small world" Mall and on the upper level of the train station on Main Street, U.S.A.

'Soundsational' is performed daily. When the park is open past 10:00pm, the parade is usually performed twice. The second parade showing is usually less busy than the first.

Paint the Night Parade

After years without a nighttime parade, Disney debuted the 'Paint the Night' Parade as part of the 60th anniversary celebrations. This has very quickly become our favorite parade at any Disney park (even beating Soundsational), and is one of the best nighttime spectaculars too. The parade lasts a lengthy 19 minutes.

Paint the Night features innovative floats, catchy tunes, dancers and many of your favorite characters. It truly is one of those parades that has to be seen to be believed.

During the parade you can see Tinker Bell, Peter Pan, Sulley and Mike (from Monster's Inc.), Lightning McQueen, Ariel, Sebastian, Flounder, Nemo, Jessie, Woody, Buzz Lightyear, Belle, Rapunzel, Cinderella, Anna and Elsa, Olaf, Goofy, Donald, Minnie and Mickey.

This parade is extremely popular and it is not uncommon to see people staking out spots 90 minutes or more in advance.

'Paint the Night' is performed daily. The parade is even shown twice per day during peak periods; when it is performed twice, the second showing is usually less busy than the first.

Top Tip: You can often combine viewings of 'Paint the Night' and 'Disneyland Forever' almost back to back and keep the same spot.

New: Starting January 11th, 2016 a new 'Paint the Night' dining package is available that includes dinner and a space in the reserved viewing areas for Paint the Night. For the three-course meal at Blue Bayou, your spot will be on Main Street, U.S.A.; for the Aladdin's Oasis dining package, your viewing spot will be located near "it's a small world".

Chapter 7

Disney California Adventure Park

Disney California Adventure, or DCA for short, is the second and newest theme park at the Disneyland Resort. However, for years after its opening, this park was nowhere near as popular as Disneyland Park. So, in 2007 Disney started working on a multi-year re-theming and expansion project for the park. This included the addition of new lands and attractions, improved theming, and a nighttime spectacular.

Nowadays, Disney California Adventure is no longer an add-on park but a full day experience with several unique attractions not found at any other Disney park worldwide – it is the perfect complement to Disneyland Park next door.

Buena Vista Street

Buena Vista Street, the entrance area of Disney California Adventure, invites guests to step into Los Angeles from the 1920s and '30s, where they experience the sights and sounds Walt Disney may have discovered when he stepped off the train in California in 1923. Buena Vista Street is named after a road with the same name in Burbank, where The Walt Disney Studios is located.

Holiday season tip: Arrive early to purchase a hand-twisted candy cane during the holiday season at Trolley Treats. These sell out quickly, and are a Disneyland tradition for many visitors.

Complimentary tour tip: Carthay Circle restaurant, the beautiful dining location on Buena Vista Street, offers a guided tour at 10:30am every day. Tours last about 15 minutes. "The Story of Carthay Circle Restaurant" teaches you about the history of the theatre that inspired the DCA building.

Attractions:
Red Car Trolley

Fastpass: No
Minimum Height: None
On-ride photo: No
Ride up and down Buena Vista Street and Hollywood Boulevard in an authentically themed red trolley.

Dining:
Clarabelle's Hand Scooped Ice Cream – Snacks, ice creams are priced at $4.50 to $14.50.
Fiddler, Fifer & Practical Café – Quick Service, sandwiches and salads are $4.50 to $10, pastries are $1.50 to $5, desserts are $3 to $6, Starbucks beverages are $2.50 to $5.50.
Carthay Circle Restaurant – Table Service, does not serve breakfast, entrees are $24 to $32 at lunch and $32-$47 at dinner, World of Color prix fixe dining package $44 per adult and $24 per child at lunch, and $67 per adult and $27 per child at dinner.
Carthay Circle Lounge – Bar lounge, snacks are $15 to $16, rolls cost $14 to $19, small plates cost $17 to $22, desserts are priced at $9 to $17. Alcoholic and non-alcoholic drinks are available.

Hollywood Land

Attractions:

For the First Time in Forever: A Frozen Sing-Along Celebration

Fastpass: No
Minimum Height: None
Show length: 30 minutes
Average wait times: Until next show starts

This show is a temporary addition to the park and has taken over from Muppet Vision 3D which used to be performed in this space. "For the First Time in Forever – A Frozen Sing-Along Celebration" transforms the old Muppet Vision 3D Theatre into the welcoming Crown Jewel Theatre of Arendelle, where Anna, Elsa and Kristoff take part in a comedic retelling of their story that features popular songs from the film.

Two Arendellian Historians, acting as hosts, lead the festivities, with the "Frozen" characters making memorable appearances throughout. Some of the favorite musical sequences (and lyrics) are shown on large screens to make sure everybody enjoys all the fun.

Muppet Vision 3D is temporarily on hiatus while this show is being performed. We expect this Frozen show to end in Late May or Early June 2016, when the new, longer and more elaborate Frozen show debuts (more information on this later).

Turtle Talk with Crush

Fastpass: No
Minimum Height: None
Show length: 15 minutes
Average wait times: Until next show

A "totally cool" show featuring Finding Nemo's turtle, Crush! This interactive show gets adults and kids alike to speak to Crush and ask him questions about the turtle world; meanwhile Crush has some questions for you about the human world. It's a whole lot of fun if you're willing to get involved. You might even learn to speak whale!

Character Close-Up

Fastpass: No
Minimum Height: None
Attraction length: Varies. Self-guided walkthrough

This walk-through exhibit allows you to see how classic animation is made, with sketches, models and even a zoetrope.

The Twilight Zone: Tower of Terror

Fastpass: Yes
Minimum Height: 40 inches (1.02m)
On-ride photo: No
Ride length: 6 minutes (ride time plus pre-show)
Average wait times: 40 to 60 minutes

The Twilight Zone: Tower of Terror transports you to another dimension dropping you 200 feet straight down - and not just once, but many times. Disney summarizes the ride nicely: "You are the passengers on a most uncommon elevator about to ascend into your very own episode of...The Twilight Zone. One stormy night long ago, five people stepped through the door of an elevator and into a nightmare. That door is opening once again, and this time it's opening for you."

You board a service elevator; learn about the ghostly past of the hotel and then experience several drops for yourself. You also can really feel the force of the elevator being pulled down faster than gravity meaning you get lifted out of your seat. It is a slightly nicer feeling than free-fall drops in our opinion. The motors on this ride are very powerful and within a split second the elevator changes from going up to down. It really is a thrill. The atmosphere inside is truly immersive and is perhaps the best theming in the whole of the Disneyland Resort.

We recommend you get a Fastpass for this one, as the queue can be long. However, please note that by using Fastpass you will miss out on a lot of the detail in the queue. We recommend that first time riders buy the photo for the priceless reactions.

Animation Academy

Fastpass: No
Minimum Height: None
Show length: 15 to 20 minutes
Average wait times: Until next show
Learn about how the Disney characters are brought to life at the Animation Academy through a show with a difference. Here, you can learn how to draw one of the characters for yourself!

Monsters, Inc. Mike & Sulley to the Rescue!

Fastpass: No
Minimum Height: None
On-ride photo: No
Ride length: 5 minutes
Average wait times: 15 to 30 minutes
This dark ride brings the story of Monsters Inc. to life with Boo's escape – see familiar scenes from the Monsters Inc. films in front of your very eyes. Due to its slow loading nature, this attraction can have long wait times when shows finish. Look out for Roz at the end who interacts with riders!

Sorcerer's Workshop

Fastpass: No
Minimum Height: None
Attraction length: Varies. Self-guided walk through
The Sorcerer's Workshop is a self-guided walkthrough exhibition made up of three different areas: Ursula's Grotto, The Beast's Library and the Magic Mirror Realm. Each has fun interactive elements to explore.

Entertainment:
Disney Junior – Live on Stage
Fastpass: No
Minimum Height: None
Show length: 25 minutes
Average wait times: Until next show
With catchy songs, puppets and a toddler-friendly environment, Disney Junior is perfectly designed with the younger members of the family in mind. Mickey, Minnie and friends from the Mickey Mouse Clubhouse make an appearance, as do characters from Jake and the Never Land Pirates, and Handy Manny. This show is highly recommended for the younger ones.

Anna & Elsa's Royal Welcome
Fastpass: Yes
In the Disney Animation building, you can meet Anna and Elsa from Disney's Frozen. The only way to meet the Frozen sisters is with a Fastpass reservation – there is no regular standby queue line, and your Fastpass return time will only be 20 minutes long. You can get Fastpasses outside the Disney Animation building. Even with a reservation, you can typically expect a wait of between 15 and 45 minutes. This Fastpass does not impact on your ability to obtain other Fastpasses at the park.

Frozen: Live at the Hyperion

Fastpass: No
Minimum Height: None
Show length: Unknown
Average wait times: Until next show
Loading: 2000 guests per show
Debuting on May 27, 2016 is a brand new show – **"Frozen: Live at the Hyperion"**. Disney says:

"This new show will immerse you in the world of "Frozen" as never before, with elaborate costumes and sets, stunning special effects and surprising scenic transformations. Our stage production of 'Frozen' will stay true to the heart and soul of the film. Anna and Elsa will carry the audience on an emotional journey that includes show-stopping production numbers and a few unique theatrical twists. We can't wait for everyone to see it!"

Dining:

Award Wieners – Quick Service, does not serve breakfast, hot dogs are $7 to $8.50.
Schmoozies – Quick Service, smoothies are $5.70, coffees are $2.50 to $4.50.
Fairfax Market – Snacks, including fruit, chips and bread are priced between $2 to $7.

A bug's land

This land is inspired by nature's creatures and has been a staple of the park since it opened in 2001. There is a larger-than-life feel in this area with giant plants that makes guests feel like small bugs.

Attractions:

In addition to the attractions that follow, you may also want to visit **Princess Dot Puddle Park**, a water play area.

Flik's Flyers

Fastpass: No
Minimum Height: None
On-ride photo: No
Ride length: 1 minute 30 seconds
Average wait times: 5 to 20 minutes
A standard spinner-style attraction like Dumbo, but themed around bugs.

Francis' Ladybug Boogie

Fastpass: No
Minimum Height: None
On-ride photo: No
Ride length: 1 minute
Average wait times: 5 to 15 minutes
A spinning teacup-style ride themed to ladybirds.

Tuck and Roll's Drive 'Em Buggies

Fastpass: No
Minimum Height: None
On-ride photo: No
Ride length: 2 minutes
Average wait times: 5 to 15 minutes
Standard bumper cars with a bug theme.

Heimlich's Chew Chew Train

Fastpass: No
Minimum Height: None
On-ride photo: No
Ride length: 2 minutes
Average wait times: 5 to 15 minutes
Hope aboard Heimlich's slow-moving train as you venture around a bug's land.

It's Tough to be a Bug!

Fastpass: No
Minimum Height: None
Show length: 10 minutes
Average wait times: Under 15 minutes
The meanest and nastiest 3D show we have ever experienced. Be prepared to see how humans treat insects and then get a taste of your own medicine. Even when you think the show is over, it's not! Warning: This attraction will frighten some adults, and may terrify children.

Cars Land

Cars Land invites guests to step right into Radiator Springs and meet all of their favorite friends from the hit Disney Pixar movies "Cars" and "Cars 2." Spanning a whopping 12 acres in Disney California Adventure Park, Cars Land is truly a must-see for anyone visiting the Disneyland Resort.

Cars Land is home to one of the largest and most elaborate attractions created for any Disney theme park, **Radiator Springs Racers**. The land opened in June 2012 and was described as the "crown jewel of our Disney California Adventure expansion" by Disney. It is our favorite area of the park.

Attractions:
Mater's Junkyard Jamboree

Fastpass: No
Minimum Height: At least 32 inches (0.81m) and accompanied by another rider at least 54 inches (1.37m) tall. Must be at least 54 inches (1.37m) tall to ride alone.
On-ride photo: No
Ride length: 2 minutes
Average wait times: 15 to 45 minutes
This ride gets you on board a little tractor that spins and dances to music, similar to a teacup-style spinning ride but with a bigger thrill. It can be surprisingly fast at times, but it is a lot of fun.

Luigi's Rollickin' Roadsters

Fastpass: No
Minimum Height: At least 32 inches (0.81m) to ride.
On-ride photo: No
Ride length: 1 minute 30 seconds
Average wait times: 30 to 60 minutes

Gear up for a spin as Luigi has set up an Italian area in Radiator Springs to celebrate race day. Hop in one of the cars and marvel as you perform one of many traditional dances to Italian music. This attraction was formerly called Luigi's Flying Tires but that attraction was completely replaced by this new attraction in early 2016.

Radiator Springs Racers

Fastpass: Yes
Minimum Height: 40 inches (1.02m)
On-ride photo: No
Ride length: 6 minutes
Average wait times: 90 to 120 minutes
Loading: 2 rows of 3 people, 6 per car. About 1500 riders per hour.
The premier attraction of the land, Radiator Springs Racers is a high-speed thrill ride through Radiator Springs and the world of 'Cars'. The indoor section of the ride truly is a technological marvel as the talking cars have been made to look extremely lifelike – Disney even created new materials in order to do this! Then, you line up and race against another car towards the finish line; you will never know who will win as the result is different every time. This ride is great fun and an absolute must do!

Fun Fact: At nearly 300,000 square feet in area, and 125 feet tall at its peak, The Ornament Valley Mountain Range in Cars Land is the largest rock structure in any Disney theme park in the USA.

Dining:

Fillmore's Taste-In – Snacks including fruit, chips and drinks, $3 to $4.50.
Cozy Cone Motel – Snacks, chili con queso is $7.50, ice cream are $4 to $5, pretzel bites are $5.50, and popcorn is $5 to $13.
Flo's V8 Café – Quick Service, entrees are $5.50 to $8.50 at breakfast, and $11 to $12.50 at lunch and dinner.

Pacific Wharf

This area resembles Monterey's Cannery Row, with hints of San Francisco's Fisherman's Wharf. It is a big place to come and eat in the park with a large variety of eateries.

Attractions:
The Bakery Tour

Fastpass: No
Minimum Height: None
Experience length: Walkthrough attraction – about 9 minutes
Average wait times: Guests are let in every 5 to 10 minutes
This is a walkthrough attraction that takes you through the history of the Boudin Bakery and lets visitors learn how bread is made for the whole of the Disneyland resort.

Dining:

Alfresco Tasting Terrace – Bar and lounge, appetizers are $7.50 to $12.50, wine flights are $18 to $25 and bottles go up to $85.
Mendocino Terrace at the Golden Vine Winery – Bar and lounge, the cheese snack box is $15, wines are $9 to $23 per glass, and beers are $6 to $7.
Wine Country Trattoria – Table Service, does not serve breakfast, entrees are $14 to $22.50 at lunch, and $16 to $22.50 at dinner. The World of Color prix-fixe dining package is priced at $30 per adult and $19 per child at lunch, and $43 per adult and $23 per child at dinner.
Ghirardelli Soda Fountain and Chocolate Shop – Quick Service, shakes and floats are $6.50 to $9, chocolate drinks are $4.50 to $9, scoop ice cream is $4.50 to $6.50, sundaes are $8 to $11, and coffees are $2 to $6.
The Lucky Fortune Cookery – Quick Service, does not serve breakfast, rice bowls with meat or tofu are priced at $11 each. Sides are $3.50 to $4.
Rita's Baja Blenders – Bar and lounge, drinks are $5.50 to $8. Serves alcoholic and non-alcoholic beverages.
Pacific Wharf Café – Quick Service, does not serve breakfast, entrees are $10 to $11 at lunch and dinner.
Cocina Cucamonga Mexican Grill – Quick Service, does not serve breakfast, entrees are $10.50 to $14.

Top Tip: Just like in San Francisco, the Ghirardelli Shop often hands out free samples as you walk in. Yum!

Paradise Pier

This area is themed around a seaside pier and contains a variety of attractions.

It is important to note that the attractions in this area of the park close early for performances of the nighttime show, 'World Of Color'. The only exception is Toy Story Midway Mania, which continues to operate as normal due to its indoor location.

Attractions:

In addition to the many attractions in the area, you may also want to check out **Games of the Boardwalk**, paid-for pier side-style games.

California Screamin'

Fastpass: Yes
Minimum Height: 48 inches (1.22m)
On-ride photo: No
Ride length: 2 minutes 30 seconds
Average wait times: 20 to 30 minutes
Loading: Rows of 2. About 2200 guests per hour

At first glance this appears to be a wooden rollercoaster, like those found on seaside piers worldwide, though closer inspection reveals a steel coaster with two lift hills, one loop and thousands of feet of track. This is one fun ride that is not to be missed.

King Triton's Carousel

Fastpass: No
Minimum Height: None
On-ride photo: No
Ride length: Under 2 minutes
Average wait times: Under 10 minutes
This is a classic carrousel just like any other, but here instead of horses you will find all kinds of sea creatures including dolphins and seals.

Toy Story Midway Mania!

Fastpass: No
Minimum Height: None
On-ride photo: No
Ride length: 5 minutes
Average wait times: 30 to 60 minutes
Loading: Rows of 2, 8 people per car.
This is an interactive shooter attraction where each passenger in the car (in pairs, sat back to back) is given a gun to shoot at interactive screens. It is great family fun and each scene is different along the way. Work hard to beat everyone else but with a frantic urge to win, you may find that your arm aches after riding.

One of the resort's most popular attractions, Midway Mania draws huge crowds whilst suffering from a low hourly capacity. The result is long lines that are rarely under 30 minutes.

Mickey's Fun Wheel

Fastpass: No
Minimum Height: None
On-ride photo: No
Ride length: 8 minutes
Average wait times: 10 to 30 minutes
Loading: 600 guests per hour
This giant Ferris wheel offers two different seating arrangements – the classic non-swinging seating areas and the more innovative (and thrilling, might we add) swinging gondolas that gather a surprising amount of speed. Fun but choose your gondola wisely – the swinging gondolas are an adventure unto themselves.

Goofy's Sky School
Fastpass: Yes
Minimum Height: 42 inches (1.07m)
On-ride photo: No
Ride length: 1 minute 30 seconds
Average wait times: 20 to 45 minutes
A small rollercoaster with tight turns themed to Goofy and his sky school. Take to the skies in this wild ride.

Top Tip: A Single Rider line is available.

Silly Symphony Swings

Fastpass: No
Minimum Height: 40 inches (1.02m) for the tandem swing, 48 inches (1.22m) for an individual swing.
On-ride photo: No
Ride length: 2 minutes
Average wait times: Under 20 minutes
A standard spinning chair ride like that found at many amusement parks – this one is themed around Disney's silly symphonies.

Top Tip: If you are in a group, choose the tandem line for shorter waits.

Golden Zephyr

Fastpass: No
Minimum Height: None
On-ride photo: No
Ride length: 2 minutes
Average wait times: Under 10 minutes
Fly in a zephyr around in circles. This is very similar to the Silly Symphony Swings attraction, but here everyone is in one vehicle instead of in separate seats. This attraction is often closed due to safety restrictions – if there is even minimal wind, the ride stops operating.

Jumpin' Jellyfish

Fastpass: No
Minimum Height: 40 inches (1.02m)
On-ride photo: No
Ride length: 1 minute
Average wait times: 5 to 15 minutes
A small kids' drop ride – as found in many parks – themed to jellyfish.

The Little Mermaid – Ariel's Undersea Adventure

Fastpass: No
Minimum Height: None
On-ride photo: No
Ride length: 6 minutes
Average wait times: Under 15 minutes
Loading: 2 or 3 guests per clamshell
Step into the undersea world as you board a clamshell and visit Ariel. The storytelling is great, the animatronics are amazing, and the ride just continues to entertain throughout while moving slowly and steadily enough to not frighten young ones. Watch out for the breathtaking appearance of Ursula.

Dining:

Ariel's Grotto – Character Dining, the breakfast buffet is $37 per adult and $20 per child, the lunch buffet is $42 per adult and $22 per child. Dinner is the World of Color prix fixe dining package (this is not a character meal) available at $43 per adult and $23 per child.
Cove Bar – Bar and lounge, appetizers are $9.50 to $15, wines are $9 to $13 per glass or $35 to $53 per bottle, sangria is $9.50. A number of other drinks are offered, including both alcoholic and non-alcoholic drinks.
Paradise Pier Ice Cream Company – Snacks, ice creams and floats are $4 to $5.
Boardwalk Pizza & Pasta – Quick Service, this location does not serve breakfast, pizzas are $7.50 to $10 per slice, or $35 for a whole pizza pie, pasta is $10 and salads are $8.50 to $10.
Paradise Garden Grill – Quick Service, this location does not serve breakfast, entrees are $8.50 to $12.
Bayside Brews – Snacks, pretzels are about $4.50, also serves alcoholic and non-alcoholic drinks.
Corn Dog Castle – Snacks, this location does not serve breakfast, snacks and entrees are $8 to $8.50.

Grizzly Peak

This area of the park contains some of the most popular attractions in the park. In 2015, this area was expanded into what previously was Condor Flats.

Attractions:
Redwood Creek Challenge Trail

Fastpass: No
Minimum Height: 42 inches (1.02m) for zip line and rock wall only.
On-ride photo: No
Attraction length: Walkthrough exploration – generally 10 to 25 minutes.
This walk-through exploration area has tons of things to do. Grab a map by the entrance and complete the activities to get sticker badges – just like the Wilderness Explorers in Up. Speaking of 'Up', Russell and Dug make regular appearances in this area to help with the Wilderness Explorer ceremony. There are rope bridges to cross, as well as a zip line, a cave, rock climbing and more to experience. It's great fun for all ages.

Grizzly River Run

Fastpass: Yes
Minimum Height: 40 inches (1.02m)
On-ride photo: No
Ride length: 6 minutes
Average wait times: 15 to 50 minutes
Board a raft on your journey along the grizzly river but be prepared for drops, waterfalls, leaks and more creative ways to get you wet. Everyone will get wet on this ride no matter where they sit. Interestingly, this is the first water ride of its kind where the 'wetness' level can be adjusted, so that during the colder months you can ride this attraction and stay dry.

Soarin' Over California

Fastpass: Yes
Minimum Height: 40 inches (1.02m)
On-ride photo: No
Ride length: 4 minutes 30 seconds
Average wait times: 20 to 50 minutes

Soarin' gives you the chance to experience what it is like to fly and hang glide over the state of California. You will see iconic California locations such as Yosemite, San Diego and the Golden Gate Bridge along the way. It is a truly immersive experience, with smells and slightly seat movement to match the action on screen. If you are scared of heights this one is most definitely not for you. The attraction recently went through a HD upgrade to improve the quality of the footage.

Important: Disney has announced that this attraction will become 'Soarin' Around the World' at some point during 2016. No longer will you only soar over California, but around the planet as you see sights such as Monument Valley and the Great Wall of China, plus many others. A date for this transition has not been given.

Dining:

Smokejumpers Grill – Quick Service, this location does not serve breakfast, entrees are $9.50 to $11.

Nighttime show:
World of Color

This $75-million nighttime spectacular is truly a mind-blowing spectacle, and we would rate it the best out of all the experiences on offer at night at the Disneyland resort, even above Fantasmic. Between one and three times every evening, Paradise Pier is immersed in a 'World of Color', made up of Mickey's fun wheel, California Screaming's loop projection area, fog, lasers, fire, HD projections and 1200 fountains. This is a truly incredible and heart-wrenching 27-minute long show that is sure to unite the whole family and leave you saying 'WOW!'.

The show uses a submersible platform that is bigger than a football field, with more than 18,000 points of control and revolutionary lighting that infuses nearly 1,200 fountains with color — making it one of the largest show systems ever built.

You will experience spray from the water fountains during certain sections of the show and if you are standing towards the front you may want to consider wearing a poncho.

Although viewing is available from all across the lagoon, the ideal location to watch it from is the tiered Paradise Park World of Color viewing area, which accommodates 4500 people. Views from outside this area are less than ideal. Free Fastpass ticket reservations are required to be admitted into this location – these are dispensed from Fastpass machines located by the Grizzly River Run Fastpass machines. On peak days these reservations will run out quickly. These are merely reservations for the show and not Fastpasses – despite using the Fastpass ticket machines, these are not really actual Fastpasses so you will still be able to grab another regular Fastpass straight away.

Even with a Fastpass you will want to turn up well before your time slot as the best spots get taken quickly as soon as guests are allowed into the viewing area. While you are waiting, keep an eye on Mickey's Fun Wheel which allows you to play a fun interactive game with your smartphone before the show starts.

If you do not get a reservation for the Paradise Park World of Color viewing area, other good areas to view the show from are in front of The Little Mermaid attraction or by the Golden Zephyr ride and do not require a reservation ticket.

If you want to become part of the action, you might want to purchase the $25 Glow with the Show products, which illuminate in time with the show.

The other way to guarantee a viewing spot is to purchase one of the World of Color dining packages from Wine Country Trattoria, Carthay Circle Restaurant, or Ariel's Grotto that include a ticket allowing you into the specially reserved central standing section of the viewing area. The World of Color prix-fixe dining package is priced at $30 per adult and $19 per child at lunch, and $43 per adult and $23 per child at dinner.

Occasionally, sequences of the show may change to incorporate new movies or for seasonal changes.

During the Christmas season, the show is replaced by a winter-themed spectacle, 'World of Color – Winter Dreams'. This show uses the same technology but bears no resemblance to the regular World of Color show. Instead the entire show reflects the holiday mood.

New: Throughout the 60th anniversary celebrations, 'World of Color' has been replaced by 'World of Color – Celebrate', a completely new show with a bigger focus on Walt Disney and his accomplishments.

Note: All viewing space for this show is standing room only with no seats.

Top Tip: When more than one show is scheduled on the same night, the later showing will be much less crowded than the first.

Live entertainment:

There is a lot of live street entertainment around the park, including appearances from popular characters and more. On Buena Vista Street, by the fountain and Carthay Circle, the **Red Car News Boys** put on a brief show inspired by the musical Newsies several times a day, including a hit number from the Broadway show – you will even get to see talking Mickey make an appearance. The **Five and Dime** also perform on Buena Vista Street – this jazz band rolls up in their 1920s inspired car and performs a few numbers.

Also, on Buena Vista Street, look out for the people who are dressed to look like they belong in the 1920s, these are the **Citizens of Buena Vista** who live here every day – meet the wacky policeman, the well-travel photographer or the hilarious bike messenger along this road. Have a chat with them.

In Paradise Bay, watch Goofy perform **Instant Concert...Just Add Water** a short 5-minute show where Maestro Goofy gets up on a podium and leads the World of Color fountains in a musical adventure. Each show throughout the day is different. By the Little Mermaid attraction you can enjoy **Fineas and Ferb's Rockin' Rollin' Dance Party**. Finally, in Cars Land you will find **DJ's Dance and Drive** street party, and in the morning you can meet and greet **Red the Firetruck**.

Parade:
Pixar Play Parade

This 12-minute Pixar-themed parade contains creative floats, a catchy song and some cool characters including some of your favorite Pixar characters from The Incredibles, Monsters University, A Bug's Life and Toy Story, as well as many others.

The parade route begins by the Boardwalk Pizza and Pasta restaurant in Paradise Pier, goes around Grizzly Peak (on the Car's Land side, not the Soarin' side), then goes onto Buena Vista Street near the fountain and then down towards the Tower of Terror where it ends. On days when there are two parade showings, the parade route may be reversed for one or both showings. The Golden Vine Winery area offers great elevated views but none of the parade route is particularly busier than other sections.

This parade is performed twice a day when the park is open late. Beware that during the summer, viewers of the parade can get very wet!

Chapter 8

Fastpass

The Disneyland Resort offers an incredible system, by the name of Fastpass, which allows you to get onto selected rides with little or no wait. This system allows you to virtually reserve a slot to experience an attraction without having to wait in line, meaning you can use that time to do something else. Fastpass is only available on a limited number of popular attractions - see them below.

List of FASTPASS attractions:
Disneyland Park:

- Autopia
- Big Thunder Mountain Railroad
- Haunted Mansion (Halloween and Holiday seasons only)
- Indiana Jones Adventure

- Fantasmic (distributed at Big Thunder Trail in Frontierland)
- Roger Rabbit's Car Toon Spin
- Space Mountain
- Splash Mountain
- Star Tours

Disney California Adventure:

- California Screamin'
- Goofy's Sky School
- Grizzly River Run
- Radiator Springs Racers (distributed by It's Tough to Be a Bug!)

- Soarin' Over California
- The Twilight Zone: Tower of Terror
- World of Color (distributed at Grizzly River Run)

How to use Fastpass at Disneyland Resort:

1. Find a ride that offers Fastpass. You can identify these by the little "FP" logo on the park maps or by signs at the ride entrance.
2. Go to the ride and check the queue time. There will be two times shown: The standard stand-by queue time (e.g. 45 minutes), and the Fastpass return time (such as 12:30-13:30).
3. If the standard queue time is short, go straight onto the ride. If it is not, then here is your chance to use the Fastpass system.
4. The Fastpass return time will display a 1-hour time window - e.g. 12:30 - 13:30. This is the time of day you will return to ride.
5. Go to the Fastpass machines located near the entrance of the attraction and enter your park ticket or annual pass into the Fastpass machine slot. This machine will scan the barcode on your ticket.

6. Pull your park ticket out and put it away safely. The machine will print a paper Fastpass telling you what time to return. This is your Fastpass reservation. The time printed on your Fastpass will be the same as what is shown on the board at the Fastpass distribution area.
7. Feel free to do whatever you want until that time - e.g. have a meal, wander around the park or experience another attraction.
8. Return to the ride during the time window shown on your Fastpass, with your Fastpass in hand and enter through the Fastpass entrance. Early and late returns cannot be accommodated. However, if you have a valid reason as to why you are late, do explain this to the Cast Member. Entry is at their discretion.
9. Hand your Fastpass to the Cast Member at the entrance who will check it. Later in the line you will be asked to surrender your Fastpass to another Cast Member. At select attractions you may give your Fastpass to a Cast Member at the entrance. Now, you can experience the attraction usually in a few minutes skipping the regular queue.

Extra tips:

- Every Disneyland ticket and annual pass includes free Fastpass access. You do not have to pay for a Fastpass for any reason.
- There are some rides where Fastpasses will run out early in the day (sometimes by midday) so make sure to get Fastpasses for these attractions as early as possible. In Disneyland Park these are: Space Mountain, Splash Mountain and Star Tours. In DCA these are: Radiator Springs Racers, World of Color, Soarin' over California and Goofy's Sky School.
- You can only hold one Fastpass at a time, with a few exceptions, see the points below for how to hold two Fastpasses at once.
- As soon as your time window opens and it is time to ride, you can pick up another Fastpass for a different attraction. E.g. You have a Fastpass to be used on Space Mountain between 2:00pm-3:00pm, it is 2:05pm. You can pick up a Fastpass for another ride such as Star Tours (nearby) from 2:00pm and then go and ride Space Mountain. This way, you are riding Space Mountain while virtually queuing for Star Tours, saving you even more time!
- If a ride is down for technical difficulties, then the Fastpass machines will be inactive until the ride is operational again. This is to prevent a flurry of people from obtaining Fastpasses at one time and using up the entire day's allocation quickly.
- There is nothing preventing one person in your party from getting everyone's Fastpasses – simply give them everyone's park tickets and

they can scan one after the other. This can be useful if the rest of your party want to ride something that you do not want to.

- There are no Fastpass return times within the first 35 minutes of park opening. That means if you get a Fastpass at 9:00am when the park opens, the earliest return time will be at 9:35am. This is because queues are short at park opening, and Fastpass is not required.
- Fastpasses cannot be obtained until park opening. So, if you have Early Entry access, you will not be able to get Fastpasses during this time. The exception to this is Fastpasses for World of Color.
- You cannot enter rides before or after the time on your Fastpass.
- Tower of Terror and Soarin' Over California have pre-show videos that you must sit through. This can add up to 15 minutes of waiting. Generally, though, with most attractions you should be on the ride in less than 5 minutes with a Fastpass. Indiana Jones also has up to a 20-minute wait from when you have surrendered your Fastpass.
- During very busy days (Christmas Day and New Year's Eve for example) you may find that Fastpasses for all rides are gone by 2:00pm or even 1:00pm.

How to get more than one Fastpass at a time:

- It is possible to hold a Fastpass to a Disney California Adventure ride and a Disneyland Park ride Fastpass at the same time. You must hold a 2-park "hopper" park ticket to do this. Ask for your hand to be stamped at the exit of the parks, so you can return later. Remember the two parks are right in front of each other.
- If your return time is more than two hours away, then you are allowed to obtain another Fastpass two hours after you picked up the first. E.g. You pick up a Fastpass at 10:00am for Space Mountain and the return time is 15:00-16:00, in this case you can get an additional new Fastpass at 12:00pm. You can always check the time of your next Fastpass on the bottom of your most recent Fastpass ticket.
- If you want a Fastpass for Radiator Springs Racers (RSR) and want an early return time, you need to go to its Fastpass machines and line up before the park officially opens. Guests are allowed in 30 minutes before the posted opening time and Cast Members can direct you to the queue line for the RSR machines. Fastpass machines will only begin operating at park opening time. Fastpasses for this ride will usually run out faster than for any other ride.
- Fastpasses for shows are not connected to the main Fastpass system, so you can have a World of Color Fastpass and a Fantasmic Fastpass at the same time, as well as all your attraction Fastpasses.

Chapter 9

Touring Plans

Follow our touring plans to save time on your trip. We know that each group has a different need, so we have come up with a variety of different touring plans based on ages, the parks you want to visit and how adventurous you want to be – simply pick the one that's best for you.

Although it is impossible to predict exactly what will happen on a given day, our experience of the parks allows us to tell you how most visitors tour the parks and how you can skip the longer queue lines by doing the opposite of what other guests are doing.

It is very important that you follow the touring plans in the given order. If you do not wish to experience a show or an attraction, simply skip that step in the plan. We strongly recommend you do not switch the order of the steps.

These touring plans are not designed for character meets or autographs. If you want to include these, you will have to swap out steps of the plans as time allows. Alternatively, for optimal touring conditions, we recommend doing character meet and greets on a separate day to the days you use the touring plans.

The Basics:

It is important to know some basics before you use any of our touring plans:

- Purchase your park tickets in advance – if you cannot, then be at the park at least one hour before opening to buy your tickets.
- Be at the park turnstiles at least 40 minutes before the official park opening time – they let guests in early almost every day and it means you will be at the front of the crowds so you can get onto the first rides with no wait.

These tips also apply to you if you are simply following your own schedule.

Disneyland Park:

Disneyland Park has dozens of attractions – although you can get a general overview of the park in a day, it is impossible to see it all. If you are limited by time, then pick our 1-day plan. If you are touring at a more leisurely pace, take a look at our 2-day plan which should be able to cover most of the park's attractions and shows at a more relaxed pace and allow you to enjoy the atmosphere more. Three days of touring will be enough to see what this park really has to offer, and allows you the time to enjoy Table Service meals and a good part of the park's entertainment offerings.

Arriving at the parks:
Our touring plans are very much dependent on you being at the park turnstiles well before the official park opening time. If you have early entry privileges, use them. Disneyland's parking complexes usually open 2 hours before the official park opening time. From the parking locations you will take a tram or shuttle to the main Disneyland entrance plaza. You go through the bag check area, where security employees ensure that no dangerous items are in your belongings (glass bottles are not allowed, for example), and then explore the two theme parks – Disneyland Park and Disney California Adventure Park.

On most days you will be allowed entry into each theme park 30 minutes before the official park opening time. In Disneyland you can explore Main Street USA and in Disney California Adventure you can explore Buena Vista Street during the first 30 minutes before the park officially opens. Cast Members will rope off the remainder of the park, preventing you from passing. At the official park opening time a fanfare is played over the speakers and the ropes to the various park areas are removed, allowing you to fully explore the entire park.

On very busy days, the park may fully open up to 30 minutes before the official park opening time. It is also possible that you may be allowed access to select attractions until the official opening time.

It is not possible to know in advance which of the opening procedures will be used on a particular day – so, get there early and make the most of it!

1- Day "As much as humanly possible" Touring Plan:
If you have one day at Disneyland Park and want to see as much as you can, then this is the plan for you. Be aware that it requires a lot of walking with minimal breaks.

Some have described this plan, as a "military operation" in the past; so, if you are not prepared to put in the work, this is not the plan for you. If you are, then you will get to see almost twice as many attractions in a day as the average guest.

If you want a more relaxed pace, take a look at our two-day plan that follows this one.

1. Proceed straight down Main Street USA, through Sleeping Beauty Castle and into Fantasyland. Ride *Peter Pan's Flight*. This ride does not have Fastpass and is one of the most popular attractions in Fantasyland, developing long queues throughout the day.
2. Ride *Finding Nemo Submarine Voyage* in Tomorrowland. This ride develops significant queues very quickly, so make sure to get over here quickly after riding Peter Pan's Flight.
3. Get a Fastpass for *Space Mountain;* you will use this later.
4. Ride *Star Tours* in Tomorrowland.
5. Ride *Buzz Lightyear Astro Blasters* in Tomorrowland. The line is constantly moving, so time should pass relatively quickly.
6. It should be time to use your *Space Mountain* Fastpass now. Ride it. If it is not yet time, then do step 7 first and then return to this step.
7. Ride the *Matterhorn Bobsleds* in Fantasyland. There are actually two queue lines as there are two identical coaster circuits running inside the mountain; pick the one with the shortest line.
8. It is now time to trek across the park. Get a Fastpass for *Indiana Jones Adventure* in Adventureland. The Fastpass machines are conveniently located by Jungle Cruise. The time of this Fastpass can vary wildly depending on attendance at the parks. You do not want to miss your slot, so feel free to move around the next few steps as necessary.
9. Get a Fastpass for *Fantasmic* if it is operating on this day. Fastpass distribution takes place along *Big Thunder Trail* in Frontierland.
10. Ride *Jungle Cruise* in Adventureland.
11. It is probably time for a late lunch. Eat at a quick service location to maximize your time in the park.
12. See the *Enchanted Tiki Room* in Adventureland.
13. Ride *it's a small world* in Fantasyland.
14. On your way to the next step get a Fastpass for *Big Thunder Mountain Railroad* in Frontierland. You can only do this once the start time of your *Indiana Jones Adventure* Fastpass begins (or after 2 hours since you got your *Indiana Jones* Fastpass, whichever is sooner).
15. It should now be time for your *Indiana Jones Adventure* Fastpass – ride this attraction.
16. Ride *Pirates of the Caribbean* in New Orleans Square.

17. Experience the *Haunted Mansion* in New Orleans Square.
18. Explore *Tarzan's Treehouse* in Adventureland. This is a walk-through attraction.
19. Check how long it has been since you got your *Big Thunder Mountain Railroad* Fastpass. If at least two hours have elapsed, get a Fastpass for *Splash Mountain* in Critter Country. If not, ride either the *Mark Twain Riverboat* or the *Sailing Ship Columbia*. If it is time for your *Big Thunder Fastpass*, use it now.
20. If you have not yet got one, get a *Splash Mountain* Fastpass now.
21. Ride *Big Thunder Mountain Railroad* if you haven't yet used your Fastpass.
22. Ride *The Many Adventure of Winnie the Pooh*.
23. Ride *Splash Mountain* using your Fastpass.
24. That's it! You have done all the major attractions. The rest of the attractions have a fairly consistent wait time of 25 minutes or less for the majority of the day. Go and enjoy them and any shows and parades you want to see too.
25. If any nighttime shows are on plan to be there at least 45 minutes before show time; why not get a snack to help pass the time?

2-Day 'Best of Disneyland Park' Touring Plan:

Day One:
1. Proceed straight down Main Street, U.S.A. and go through the Sleeping Beauty Castle. Ride *Peter Pan's Flight* in Fantasyland.
2. Ride *Mr. Toad's Wild Ride* right next door.
3. Now, continue towards the middle of Fantasyland and ride *Dumbo*.
4. Ride *Alice in Wonderland* in Fantasyland.
5. Experience the *Storybook Land Canal Boats*, also in Fantasyland.
6. Check when the show times are for the next performance of any of the shows – we recommend you watch *Mickey and the Magical Map*. Work this around the rest of your day.
7. Get a Fastpass for *Indiana Jones Adventure* in Adventureland.
8. Get a Fastpass for *Fantasmic* if it is operating on this day. Fastpass distribution takes place along *Big Thunder Trail* in Frontierland.
9. Ride *Pirates of the Caribbean* in New Orleans Square.
10. Experience *Haunted Mansion* in New Orleans Square.
11. Check how long it is until your *Indiana Jones Adventure* Fastpass can be used. If it is time, ride it now. If not, have lunch while you wait.
12. Ride *Indiana Jones Adventure* using the Fastpass you got earlier.
13. Get a Fastpass for *Big Thunder Mountain* in Frontierland.
14. Do a circular tour on the *Disneyland Railroad* from the station in New Orleans Square, and come back to the same station.

15. Ride *The Many Adventures of Winnie the Pooh* in Critter Country
16. Experience the *Enchanted Tiki Room* in Adventureland.
17. Queue lines for attractions should be at their longest now, so take in a show or a parade if you have not yet done so.
18. Use your *Big Thunder Mountain Railroad* Fastpass.
19. Experience *Jungle Cruise* in Adventureland.
20. If there is a nighttime show performing tonight, experience either *Fantasmic*, *Paint the Night*, or the nighttime fireworks. If the park is open late the second showing of *Fantasmic* will be significantly less busy than the first.

Day Two:
1. Head straight to *Finding Nemo Submarine Voyage* in Tomorrowland.
2. Get a Fastpass for *Autopia* in Tomorrowland.
3. Ride *Matterhorn Bobsleds* in Fantasyland.
4. Ride *Astro Orbiter*.
5. Ride *Buzz Lightyear Astro Blasters*.
6. Get a Fastpass for *Space Mountain* on the way to *Autopia*.
7. Ride *Autopia* using the Fastpass you got earlier.
8. If you want to meet the characters, head over to *Mickey's Toontown* and meet Mickey, Minnie, Pluto and friends. This may take up to two hours. Stay alert for the time of your *Space Mountain* Fastpass!
9. Get a Fastpass for *Roger Rabbit's Car Toon Spin* in Mickey's Toontown.
10. Head over to Tomorrowland and ride *Space Mountain* with the Fastpass you got earlier.
11. Grab a Fastpass for *Star Tours: The Adventures Continue*.
12. It is probably time for lunch now. Have lunch and then watch *Captain* EO in Tomorrowland.
13. Head over to Mickey's Toontown again and ride *Gadget Go Coaster*.
14. Ride *Roger Rabbit's Car Toon Spin*.
15. See if *Mickey and the Magical Map* is performing. If so, see the next performance. Fit this around a visit to *it's a small world* in Fantasyland.
16. Ride the *Snow White* and *Pinocchio* rides in Fantasyland.
17. Ride *Casey Junior* in Fantasyland.
18. Those are all the major attractions done. Feel free to ride any attractions you have missed, watch parades, shows and nighttime spectaculars. Don't forget to use your *Star Tours* Fastpass. Enjoy!

Disney California Adventure:

This theme park has been re-developed over the last decade and it now has a lot to offer visitors, including many unique rides and experiences. Having said this, the attraction and entertainment roster is still nowhere near as large as at Disneyland Park.

The park can be done in a day fairly easily, provided you follow our touring plans. Otherwise, allocating one and a half days will enable you to see the park in a more leisurely way.

Make sure to check whether the theme park has early entry on the day of your visit. Early entry is held on Sundays, Mondays, Wednesdays and Fridays for hotel guests only. It is sometimes held daily during peak season. Try and avoid using the plan on days when early entry is offered — if you must, skip all the Cars Land steps and do Cars Land at the end of the day when it will be less crowded.

Note: Be prepared for a late lunch with our touring plan.

One Day Touring Plan
1. In order to achieve this touring plan, it is imperative that you are at the park turnstiles 45 minutes before the official park opening time. Usually about 30 minutes before the official park opening time, you will be allowed entry into Buena Vista Street.
2. Walk down Buena Vista Street until you reach the Carthay Circle restaurant. Here Cast Members will clearly point out the line for Fastpass tickets for Radiator Springs Racers (RSR). This line can be long, but it is worth the wait. If you get to the park early, you may be able to get a RSR Fastpass within just a few minutes.
3. At park opening time, Fastpass distribution begins for *Radiator Springs Racers*. Get a Fastpass. If there are multiple people in your party, send someone to get Fastpasses for *World of Color* with all the park tickets while another person waits in the line for the Radiator Springs Racers Fastpasses. They must get back before you reach the front of the Radiator Springs Racers Fastpass line.
4. Now proceed to *Mater's Junkyard Jamboree* in Cars Land. Ride it. While everyone is darting for *Radiator Springs* they will walk right past this gem.
5. Next in Cars Land, it's time for a ride on *Luigi's Rollickin' Roadsters*. The same thought process as above applies.
6. Cars Land should by now be very busy with the wait time for Radiator Springs Racers being at least 60 minutes. If it is time to use

your *Radiator Springs Racers* Fastpass, do so now. If not, be sure to fit it in in-between the next steps.

7. Walk over to Grizzly River Run's Fastpass area; get a Fastpass for *World of Color* from this area if you did not do this earlier.

8. Head to Hollywood Land and get a Fastpass for *The Twilight Zone: Tower of Terror*. You will only be able to do this if two hours have elapsed since you got your *Radiator Springs Racers* Fastpass, or if you have already used that Fastpass.

9. While waiting for your *Tower of Terror* Fastpass return time, head across the park to *Toy Story Midway Mania* in Paradise Pier. Ride it.

10. Ride *California Screamin'*.

11. Ride *Goofy's Sky School* in Paradise Pier.

12. Ride the other little rides near Goofy's Sky School – *Jumpin' Jellyfish, Golden Zephyr* and *Silly Symphony Swings*, until it is time for your *Tower of Terror* Fastpass.

13. Ride *Tower of Terror* using your Fastpass.

14. Walk over to *Soarin'*. Get a Fastpass.

15. It is time for a late lunch – go to a quick service location to maximize your time.

16. While waiting for your Fastpass return time for *Soarin'*, go and watch *Frozen: Live at the Hyperion*.

17. Get a Fastpass for *Grizzly River Run*.

18. Explore a bug's land and its attractions – *Flik's Flyers, Francis Ladybug's Boogie, Tuck and Roll's Drive 'Em Buggies, Heimlich's Chew Chew Train* and *It's Tough to be a Bug*. You should be able to do most of these rides and see the show within this land in less than 90 minutes.

19. Ride *Grizzly River Run* using your Fastpass.

20. Explore the *Redwood Creek Challenge Trail*

21. Ride *The Little Mermaid – Ariel's Undersea Adventure*.

22. That is the end of the plan. Ride anything you missed. If there is a parade performing, do not miss that either.

23. Do not miss the nighttime showing of *World of Color* – with your Fastpass ticket you got earlier, you can get into the reserved standing area! Remember to get there early, even with the Fastpass, for a good view.

Chapter 10
Downtown Disney:

With live entertainment, lush landscaping and innovative architecture, Downtown Disney is the ideal location for a shopping spree, a dining excursion or simply a stroll through a unique Disney-made environment.

Downtown Disney, a public esplanade leading to the entrances of Disneyland and Disney California Adventure Park, offers a lively, colorful array of innovative restaurants, interesting shops and dynamic entertainment venues.

Downtown Disney features over 50 shops, restaurants, boutiques and snack locations, plus a travel center with offices of the Walt Disney Travel Company, Travelex and Alamo Rent-A-Car. With a diverse menu of unique retail, dining and entertainment options, this place offers something for everyone. There is no charge to enter Downtown Disney.

Dining:
- **Catal Restaurant** and **Uva Bar** (Table Service, dinner only, entrees are $23 to $40) – World-renowned chef Joachim Splichal, known for his European-influenced fine cuisine, presents Catal Restaurant & Uva Bar. The two-story restaurant serves the flavors of the Mediterranean in a relaxing and chic environment.
- **Crossroads at House of Blues** (Table Service, does not serve breakfast, entrees are $15 to $29.50) – See entertainment section.
- **Earl of Sandwich** (Quick Service, breakfast hot sandwiches are $3 to $4 and omelets are $7, lunch and dinner sandwiches are $6 to $7) – Signature hot sandwiches are served for breakfast, lunch and dinner at this restaurant, founded by a direct descendent of John Montague, the

earl who invented the sandwich in 1792. Soups, salads, wraps, pastries and desserts are also on the menu.

- **ESPN Zone** (Table Service, does not serve breakfast, entrees are $13 to $28) – See entertainment section.
- **Haagen-Dazs** (Snacks, ice creams and desserts start from $4 to $8) – Famous premium ice cream, frozen yogurt, sorbet, brownies, cookies, soft drinks, juices and specialty coffee drinks.
- **Jamba Juice** (Snacks, smoothies are $5 to $7) – Celebrates the flavors of life with healthy and refreshing smoothies and juices.
- **La Brea Bakery Café** (Table Service, brunch entrees are $10 to $17, entrees are $12 to $28 at dinner) – Known throughout LA for its unique breads and pastries. Take-out also available at the 'Express' quick service location.
- **Naples Ristorante e Pizzeria** (Table Service, does not serve breakfast, entrees are $14 to $24, family sized pizzas are also available for $45) – Brings an authentic taste of Southern Italy to Downtown Disney. The restaurant features an open kitchen in which diners can observe the preparation of a variety of Italian dishes, including pizza baked in wood-burning ovens.
- **Napolini** (Quick Service, breakfast sandwiches are $9, lunch and dinner entrees are $6 to $9) – A gourmet Italian deli offering fresh salads, pastas, pizzas and sandwiches.
- **Rainforest Café** (Table Service, breakfast entrees are $9 to $15, entrees are $14 to $28 at lunch and dinner) – A highly-themed rainforest-style eating location.
- **Ralph Brennan's Jazz Kitchen** (Table Service, brunch entrees are $15 to $18, entrees are $14 to $18 at lunch and $24 to $38 at dinner) – An 'Express' quick service location is also available here. See entertainment section.
- **Starbucks** (Snack, serves breakfast items, pastries, sandwiches, coffees and other hot and cold drinks)
- **The Voodoo Lounge at House of Blues** (Bar and lounge and Table Service, appetizers are $6 to $16, entrees are $13 to $30, alcoholic and non alcoholic drinks are available) – See entertainment section.
- **Tortilla Jo's** (Table Service, does not serve breakfast, entrees are $15 to $23) and **Tortilla Jo's Taqueria** (Quick Service and bar and lounge, breakfast items are $4 to $6.50, lunch and dinner entrees are $6.50 to $9, serves alcoholic and non alcoholic drinks) – Showcases traditional Mexican dishes, strolling mariachis playing folk ballads and an outdoor cantina serving margaritas and sangrias.
- **Wetzel's Pretzels** (Snacks, pretzels and cheese dogs are $4 to $5, serves frozen and fresh drinks priced at $3 to $4.50) – This state-of-the-

art pretzel house offers a world-class selection of pretzels, dips and beverages.

Entertainment:

- **AMC Downtown Disney 12 Theatres** – A 12-screen, Art Deco inspired theater, including an IMAX screen and stadium-style seating.
- **ESPN Zone Sports Arena** – The ultimate sports dining and entertainment destination. The Zone is composed of three distinct areas: the Studio Grill, serving great American grill food; the Screening Room, offering any game on the air in the ultimate sports-viewing environment; and the Sports Arena, which challenges fans with the latest in interactive and competitive attractions.
- **House of Blues Stage** – This location offers a unique twist on its blues-jazz based restaurant and club, featuring Delta-inspired cuisine and a variety of music.
- **Ralph Brennan's Jazz Kitchen – Flambeaux's Jazz Club** – Combining a spicy mix of traditional New Orleans cuisine and hot jazz, a tradition in the New Orleans' fine-dining restaurant scene.

Shops:

- **Alamo Rent a Car** – Get a rental car in the heart of Disneyland.
- **Anna and Elsa's Boutique** – Undergo a magical transformation at this wintry salon where you can become a princess or a snowman, and revel in a flurry of *Frozen* fun all year long. Transformations start at $34.95 plus tax.
- **Apricot Lane Boutique** – Fashionable, brand name clothing.
- **Best Buy Kiosk** – Self-service kiosks offer a convenient way of buying electronics such as cameras and headphones at Best Buy prices.
- **Build-A-Bear Workshop** – Guests create their own stuffed animals as they "choose, stuff, stitch, fluff, name and dress" their way through a series of bear-making stations.
- **Disney's Pin Traders** – The premier location to buy and trade pins and to expand your collection.
- **Disney Vault 28** – This couture boutique features headlining designs from Mighty Fine, Tank Farm and Harajuku Lovers. Here you will find the hottest handbags, jewelry and apparel.
- **D-Street** – A fusion of urban style with a Disney twist, D Street is the place to find modern and cutting-edge apparel, Star Wars and Marvel product and other pop culture novelties. D Street is also considered the flagship location for Vinylmation figures and collectibles.
- **ESPN Zone Studio Store** – See entertainment section.

- **Fossil** – Get a polished retro look from a variety of wallets, purses and classic Fossil watches.
- **House of Blues Store** – See entertainment section.
- **LittleMissMatched** – Mix-and-match a variety of unique sock options, as well as totes, pajamas, hair accessories and t-shirts. Solving the mystery of the lost sock, all socks come in threes!
- **Pearl Factory** – Create your own authentic pearl jewelry at the Pearl Factory, Hawaii's Original Pearl-in-the-Oyster. This unique kiosk features more than 135 jewelry mountings for your one-of-a-kind treasure.
- **Quiksilver** – Offers hundreds of stylish goods from leading designers such as Billabong, Hurley, Ripcurl, Oakley and more.
- **Marceline's Confectionery** – Named for Marceline, Missouri, where Walt Disney grew up, this nostalgic sweet shop delivers "a spoonful of sugar" in a big way with hand-crafted signature items created by a talented team of Disney candy makers. Guest favorites include caramel apples, chocolate-covered strawberries and marshmallow treats.
- **Rainforest Café Retail Shopping Village** – "A Wild Place to Shop and Eat" offers distinctive food, entertainment and unique shopping in a tropical rain forest setting featuring a combination of live and animated wildlife, and other special effects.
- **RIDEMAKERZ** – Design a custom ride. Choose from hundreds of options to style your ride from body types, wheels, colors and accessories.
- **Sanuk** – Stylish and innovative footwear for the outdoor community.
- **Sephora** – This specialty store, originated in France, offers countless fragrances and cosmetics, with demonstrations on how to apply them.
- **Something Silver** – A first-of-its-kind shop in California, this venue features a collection of silver jewelry that is out of the ordinary.
- **Sunglass Icon** – Allow certified sun fashion consultants to select the perfect style for you. Choose from a variety of designers including Chanel, Oliver Peoples, Gucci, Oakley and more.
- **The LEGO Store** – This store offers a huge variety of the latest Lego imagination products that enable children to create and build.
- **WonderGround Gallery** – Distinct and eclectic, this uncommon art gallery provides the ultimate creative space with surprising original and limited edition art collections, and lifestyle décor.
- **Walt Disney Travel Company Guest Services**
- **World of Disney** – At 40,000 square-feet, World of Disney at Downtown Disney is one of the biggest Disney shopping experiences on earth. It offers an incredible selection of Disney toys, souvenirs, accessories and collectibles in a variety of colorful and imaginatively decorated themed shopping areas.

Chapter 11

Guests with Disabilities

Disney wants its guests to have the most enjoyable visit possible, regardless of physical or mental ability. As such, the Disneyland Resort has many accommodations for guests with disabilities who are visiting.

Mobility:

The Disneyland Resort strives to provide mainstream access whenever possible; that is, all guests utilize the main entrance to shows and attractions. However, accessibility varies from attraction to attraction within Disney Parks. Disabled guests should ask the Cast Member at the entrance to an attraction or show for the correct entrance. Sometimes guests will be able to use their ECVs, other times they must transfer to a wheelchair, and other times still they must transfer to a ride vehicle.

If your group needs to rent a wheelchair, or ECV/motorized scooter for the day, proceed to the rental location located to the right hand side of the turnstiles of Disneyland Park, outside the park itself. This is the only place to rent these items throughout the resort. Guests may bring their own into the parks.

If someone in your group with a disability needs to remain in a stroller while in the attraction queues, visit the Guest Relations lobby location near the entrance at any of the two theme parks to receive a "stroller as wheelchair" tag to be placed on your stroller.

Wheelchairs and ECVs rented at Disneyland Resort must be returned before exiting the main Disneyland area and are not permitted in the Downtown Disney area. There are a limited number of wheelchairs available for rental at select Disney Resort hotels; these rentals can usually be kept for your entire stay.

Pricing is $12 per day for a wheelchair rental in the theme parks. You can, of course, use the same rental wheelchair to go between the parks. Multi-day rentals are also available at $10 per day. Wheelchairs from resort hotels are complimentary, with a $315 refundable deposit. ECV rentals are priced at $50 per day, plus a $20 refundable deposit in the theme parks.

Guests must be at least 18 years of age to operate ECVs and a photo ID is required to rent vehicles. The maximum weight for an ECV is 450 pounds. The maximum weight for a manual wheelchair is 350 pounds. Wheelchairs and vehicles are not designed to hold more than one person.

Guests are also invited to bring and use their own ECVs and wheelchairs throughout the Disneyland Resort. Rented wheelchairs and rented ECVs are not permitted in the Downtown Disney area.

Hearing:
Guests with hearing disabilities have the following accommodations for them at the theme parks: Assistive Listening systems, Reflective Captioning, Sign Language interpretation, Text Typewriter telephones, Handheld Captioning, Video Captioning and written aids.

Some attractions are equipped with reflective captioning – simply inform the attractions Cast Members at the attraction if you need this, so that they can enable it.

Visual:
Guests with hearing disabilities have the following accommodations for them at the theme parks: Audio Description devices (which describe over twenty of the park's attractions), Braille guidebooks and digital audio tours.

Disability Access Service (DAS) Card:
The Disability Access Service (DAS) Card is designed for any guest with a disability (including non-apparent disabilities) who is not able to wait in a normal queue line, and their party. The total party size including the disabled guest is 6 people. This can be extended when talking to a Cast Member. DAS Cards can be obtained from Guest Relations at each theme park – no proof of disability is required but the Cast Member will ask you several screening questions to determine whether the DAS Card is appropriate for you.

How does the system work?
A DAS Card-holding guest goes to one of the Guest Relations kiosks located throughout the park and asks the Cast Member there to use the DAS Card system for a particular ride. They will need their own park ticket, as well as those for all members of the group who will be riding along with the DAS Card-holding guest.

The Cast Member will look at the current wait time for the attraction you wish to ride and issue the guest with a return time. The return time will be the current wait minus 10 minutes. E.g. it is 2:00pm and the wait time for an attraction is 45 minutes – the guest will be issued with a 2:35pm return time.

Until the return time, the guest can do whatever they wish. They can then ride the attraction any time after the return time reservation, not necessarily at exact time, so a guest could use a 2:45pm return time at 3:00pm or 4:00pm.

Only one return time may be active at once – once it has been used, another return time can be made for another attraction. The system can be combined with Fastpass to increase the number of attractions visited per day.

A guest whose disability is based on the necessity to use a wheelchair or scooter does not need a DAS Card. Depending on the attraction, the guest will either wait in the standard queue or receive a return time at the attraction based on the current wait time.

Those who are visiting on trips organized by wish granting organizations and children with life-threatening illnesses have a separate program in place.

Disney says any guest who feels this system will not work for them should see Guest Relations to work out a solution.

At the resort hotels:
Some examples of accommodations that are offered in resort hotels include: wheelchair-accessible bathrooms, wheelchair-accessible ramps and elevators, rooms designed for hearing impaired Guests and rooms that accommodate service animals. Accessible rooms can be booked online by using the "Accessible room" filter, or by calling (714) 520-5045 to discuss requirements in more detail.

Accommodations at the Disneyland Resort for guests with disabilities:

- Rental wheelchairs
- Rental ECVs
- Accommodations for service animals – including relief areas.
- Assistive Listening systems
- Reflective Captioning

- Sign Language interpretation
- Text Typewriter telephones
- Handheld Captioning
- Video Captioning
- Audio Description devices
- Braille guidebooks
- Digital audio tours

What about specifics?
If you require specific information regarding details of each attraction, we strongly recommend you see Disneyland Resort's useful guide here - **https://secure.cdn1.wdpromedia.com/media/dlr_v0200/en_US/help/ Disneyland_Guide_For_Guests_With_Cognitive_Disabilities.pdf**.

Chapter 12

Meeting the Characters:

For many, a visit to the Disneyland Resort is not complete without meeting some of the characters in the parks. After all, these are the characters many people have grown up with, and meeting them in real life can be a real dream come true.

This chapter is for those who want to make a stop to see some of them. In total there are about sixty characters that meet in the parks throughout the day. Character meets have evolved greatly over the past few years and experiences now vary – some are 'random' character appearances which are not publicized on the park schedule, others are 'scheduled' meet and greets where you queue and take a photo, and others are more elaborate indoor experiences. You can also meet characters at select dining experiences.

If you ever need help finding a particular character, simply ask a Cast Member to find out when a character will next be out. They can usually find out the whereabouts of any character for you! Here we have detailed character appearances that happen regularly and usually on a daily basis.

Character Locations:

Unfortunately, you will not find characters roaming in the plaza area between the theme parks, in Downtown Disney or in the hotels (except at paid-for character dining experiences). That means that you will find all the characters in the two theme parks. Below is a list of where certain characters usually meet – the characters are rarely (with the exception of the characters in Mickey's Toontown) available all day and come and go throughout the day. Character locations may change without notice.

Disneyland Park:
- **Aladdin** – In Adventureland
- **Alice and the Mad Hatter** (and friends) – In Fantasyland and/or by the piano at the Coca Cola Refreshment Corner.
- **Ariel** – Fantasy Faire area
- **Aurora** – Fantasy Faire area
- **Belle** – Fantasy Faire area
- **Cinderella** – Fantasy Faire area
- **Donald** – In Mickey's Toontown
- **Goofy** – Either in Frontierland or Mickey's Toontown
- **Jasmine** – In Adventureland
- **Merida** (from 'Brave') – In Fantasyland in front of it's a small world

- **Mickey** – In Mickey's Toontown at his house
- **Minnie** – In Mickey's Toontown at her house
- **Pluto** – In Mickey's Toontown
- **Pooh** – In Critter Country by the Winnie the Pooh attraction
- **Princess Tiana** ('Princess and the Frog') – In New Orleans Square
- **Rapunzel** – Fantasy Faire area
- **Snow White** – Near her wishing well in the castle courtyard area
- **Tigger** – In Critter Country by the Winnie the Pooh attraction
- **Tinker Bell** (and friends) – At the Pixie Hollow area to the right of the castle

You will also commonly find a few characters in Town Square by the park entrance after the train station, and on the hub in front of the castle.

Disney California Adventure:
- **Anna, Elsa & Olaf** – At Animation Academy, in Hollywood Land
- **Ariel (and friends)** – Ariel's Grotto restaurant
- **Atta** (from 'A Bug's Life') – In A Bug's Land
- **Captain America** and **Spider-Man** – Hollywood Land
- **Duffy** the Disney Bear – Opposite Ariel's Grotto restaurant
- **Donald** – Opposite Ariel's Grotto restaurant
- **Doug** (from 'Up') – At the Redwood Creek Challenge Trail
- **Flik** (from 'A Bug's Life') – In A Bug's Land
- **Lightning McQueen** (from 'Cars') – Cozy Cone Motel, Cars Land
- **Mater** (from 'Cars') – Cozy Cone Motel, Cars Land
- **Oswald the Lucky Rabbit** – On Buena Vista Street
- **Russell** (from 'Up') – At the Redwood Creek Challenge Trail
- **The Incredibles** – Hollywood Land

Character Dining:

If you want to combine eating with meeting the characters, then character dining experiences are a great option for you. You will not even need to wait in line to meet the characters as they come round to every table.

In our opinion, the food is not usually the best at these types of places, though it is definitely not bad. However, you are definitely paying more for the entertainment than for high-class food.

Character dining experiences are all buffet style or family style meals allowing you to pick and choose what you eat. Adult prices are for guests aged 10 and up, and child prices are for guests aged 3 to 9. All prices exclude tax.

There are several character dining experiences:

- **Ariel's Disney Princess Celebration** – At Ariel's Grotto in Disney California Adventure. Characters at breakfast and lunch only (last seating at 3:55pm). Breakfast is priced at $37 for adults and $20 for children. Lunch is priced at $42 for adults and $22 for children.
- **Disney's PCH Grill** – At the Paradise Pier Hotel. The 'Surf's Up Breakfast' is served from 7:00am to 11:00am. It is priced at $31 for adults and $16 for children.
- **Goofy's Kitchen** – At the Disneyland Hotel. Character breakfast (7:00am to 12:00pm on weekdays and 7:00am to 2:00pm on weekends) and dinner (5:00pm to 9:00pm) only. Breakfast is priced at $31 for adults and $16 for children. Dinner is priced at $39 and $23 respectively.
- **Plaza Inn** – On Main Street, U.S.A. in Disneyland Park. Character breakfast until 11:00am. Priced at $30 for adults and $14 for children.
- **Storyteller's Café** – At the Grand Californian Hotel. Breakfast buffet only (from 7:00am to 11:00am). Priced at $30 for adults and $15 for children. This breakfast also offers additional items to order a la carte, these are charged at between $7.50 and $23 each.

Character Meeting Tips:

- Character wait times can be as long as, or longer than, the wait times for popular rides. So, do be prepared to wait.
- Do not force children to interact with characters. If they are scared, console them, even if you have waited 30 minutes to meet Mickey. Being next to a five-foot mouse would be scary for anyone that age.
- For the face characters (the ones who speak), chat to them and get an insight into their lives – this can make for some great memories.
- There are many more characters out earlier in the day, during mornings and early afternoons, than in the evenings.
- Characters can have limited vision. Be aware of their blind spots and that they might not be able to see what is happening to their side, or even right in front of them.
- Characters can sign anything – not just autograph books. They will not however sign anything you are wearing on your person.
- Character Attendant Cast Members will happily assist and take photos; they will be present with most characters.
- Characters cannot hold children or infants, so please do not ask.
- Follow the character attendants' instructions and do not be angry if the character needs to go for a quick break before your turn.
- Some characters cannot talk – no matter how hard you try.
- Be courteous to the characters – do not step on, or hurt, a character.

Chapter 13

Doing Disney on a budget

Although visiting the Disneyland Resort is not exactly cheap, it can be done on a budget and you can still have a fantastic trip whil saving some cash along the way. Follow these tips and reap the savings!

Traveling to the Disneyland Resort:

Driving – If you are located in the United States, or a country connected to it by land, driving can be a good option and save you a lot of money compared to flying. Remember to factor in the price of tolls and gas. This can be especially economical for larger groups.

Budget flights – Starting at under $100, these can be great value if booked far enough in advance. Also watch out for last minute sales. Or use your loyalty points!

Planning:

1. Hotels – Do you really need an on-site Disney hotel? They are nice and convenient but can be much more expensive than off-site hotels. Remember to factor in other costs like resort fees, taxes, parking charges and transport costs before opting for an off-site hotel. Many hotels are located within walking distance of the Disneyland Resort. We recommend you book offsite, due to the huge savings– you could then use some of the savings to treat yourself to a nice meal or a guided tour of the parks. The savings for the hotel alone may even be enough to pay for your park tickets or airfare.

We did a test booking as an example to show you how much you can really save. In this example we are booking stays of 3 nights for two adults and two children staying Thursday 7th April to Sunday 10th April 2016.

We only looked at hotels within a radius of 0.5miles. Room prices varied from $328 total including taxes and fees for a 2-star hotel to $524 for a 3-star hotel. The closest 4-star hotel (Anaheim Marriott Hotel) is 0.78 miles away and priced at $596. These prices are for the entire length of stay.

In comparison, a stay at the Disney resort hotels was much more expensive: Paradise Pier Hotel - $1155 (3.5 stars), Disneyland Hotel - $1583 (4 stars), and Grand Californian Hotel and Spa - $1872 (4.5 stars). There you go – an incredible difference in price between staying at a Disney hotel and at a non-Disney hotel. The 4-star Marriott offers many of the same amenities as the Disneyland Hotel, yet is almost a third of the price.

2. **Buy an annual pass** – If you plan on visiting more than twice in the same year, buying an annual pass can be a money-saver. Especially if staying off-site and driving, as you will not need to pay for parking each day. It can also save you a lot on rooms, dining and merchandise.

3. **Wait for a special offer** – The Disneyland Resort often runs special offers – whether it is discounted room prices or free nights, make sure you keep a look out for these.

4. **Downgrade your hotel** – Do you really need a luxurious Disney hotel? Will you ever use the extra amenities you are paying for at the Grand Californian? If not, but you still want to stay on property, then downgrade to somewhere like the Paradise Pier Hotel. The best way to save money is, of course, to stay off property.

5. **Tickets** – Pre-purchase tickets online at reputable websites such as CheapTickets (www.cheaptickets.com) and aRes (**http://arestravel.com**). There can be savings of over $50 per person. In addition, Canadian, Australian and New Zealand visitors should take advantage of the special tickets available to them. See our tickets chapter for more details.

6. **Quieter times** – By visiting when the parks are less busy, you will be able to do more each day so you can spend fewer days in the parks. Hotel prices will also be cheaper and dining prices can be marginally cheaper too. For a good guide, avoid the days that are blockout dates on annual passes – they will be busier.

At the Parks:

1. **Packed lunches** – You can make your own packed lunches such as sandwiches, and take them into the parks. Due to the Disneyland Resort being located in the middle of a town, you can just walk or drive to a supermarket – buy food, and make snacks or meals in your hotel room or condo.

2. **Eat meals off-site** – Once you leave Disney-owned land, there are places to eat in every direction you look – and at more reasonable prices, not prices inflated at two or three times like at Disneyland.

3. **Have table service meals at lunch** – Table Service meals and buffet meals can be substantially cheaper at lunch than at dinner. Sometimes the food on offer is different; sometimes it is exactly the same.

4. **Take your own photos** – If you do not want to pay $15 or $20 for a character photo, take one yourself with your own camera or ask a Cast Member to do it for you. The Cast Members are happy to help.

5. **Take your own costumes/plushes** – If your little boy or girl wants to buy a dress or outfit in the parks then there is a way that you can save money. These items are substantially cheaper online, at supermarkets or anywhere off Disneyland Resort property. Just buy them and pack them secretly. Give your child the costume once you arrive and they will be over the moon. The same applies to Disney plushes and toys.

6. **More affordable meals** – Although dining at the resort is expensive, some restaurants offer better value than others. Kids meals in particular are much better value than adult meals in our opinion. Remember that if you do not want fries with a meal, they can be removed saving you money – everything can be ordered a la carte. Or, alternatively, have a late lunch buffet and then just have a smaller snack for dinner.

7. **Use Fastpass** – See our whole chapter dedicated to this service. It will save you hours of queuing time in lines, meaning you can spend fewer days in the park and save on food and park ticket costs.

Chapter 14

Dining:

There is a huge variety of places to eat at the Disneyland Resort, from sandwiches to fast food, to table service dining and even character buffet options.

Top Tip: You do not have to order from the set menu, although it may save you money if you do. Ordering an item separately is completely fine.

The basics – restaurant types:

Buffet restaurants – 'All you can eat' food. Just fill up your plate from all the food offered, as often as you want. A variation on buffets are "family style" meals where you do not pick up the food yourself but instead servers come around and give out food as you ask for it.

Quick Service – Fast food. Order your meal and it will be with you in a minute or two. Everything from burgers and chips, to chicken, to pizza and pasta.

Table service – These are restaurants where you order from a menu, and a server brings you your food.

Character buffets – These are all-you-can eat places where characters come around to interact with you and take photos while you eat.

A quick note:

Prices at the Disneyland Resort are inflated – there is no doubt about it. The moment you step foot onto the Disneyland Resort, whether it be in the hotels, in Downtown Disney or inside the theme parks, you are signing a virtual contract that allows you to 'enjoy Disney prices' where you may pay up to three or four times what you would pay outside the resort. Keep this in mind when looking through menus.

This will, however, come as no surprise to theme park veterans who are accustomed to inflated prices. Those visiting from outside the US, may still be pleasantly surprised by how much more affordable food is at theme parks here than elsewhere.

Reservations and cancellations:

In order to eat at Table Service restaurants, reservations are recommended but not required. These can be made on the day, or a few days in advance, depending on how busy the season is.

This is a far cry from the Walt Disney World Resort where restaurant reservations are made 180 days in advance with little chance of securing certain oversubscribed dining locations.

Dining reservations can be made over the phone at 714-781-3463 and then selecting option 4. Reservations can be made up to 60 days in advance for any restaurant at the Disneyland Resort, except Rainforest Café that handles its own bookings at 714-772-0413. Reservations can also be made online for all restaurants at **https://disneyland.disney.go.com/dining/**.

If you are in the theme parks, you can also approach the podium at the entrance of any restaurant and make a reservation for later in the day or over the following days, including making reservations for other restaurants.

A reservation for a certain time does not guarantee you immediate seating – your wait may be up to 20 minutes. If you know that you wish to dine at a certain location, we recommend you make a reservation as early as possible to avoid disappointment. Do not rely on being at the resort before making your reservation.

A credit or debit card is required when making a table service reservation. Cancellations for restaurants should be made the day before, by 11:59pm. If cancellations are not made by this time, a $10 per person charge will apply for no-shows. Cancellations can be made by calling the reservations line at 714-781-3463.

Dress code:

At all the theme park restaurants, the dress code is simply what you would wear in the theme parks – whether that is a shirt or a tank top.

Resort restaurants, such as Napa Rose, have a business casual dress code:

Men's dress code: Dress slacks, jeans, trousers, or dress shorts, short- or long-sleeved shirt with a collar or t-shirt required. Jackets are optional.
Ladies dress code: Jeans, skirt, or dress shorts with blouse, sweater or t-shirt, or a dress required.
Not permitted: Tank tops, swimsuits or swimsuit cover-ups, hats for men, cut offs, torn clothing of any kind, or t-shirts with offensive language and/or graphics.

Additional notes and tips:
- Ages 3 to 9 are considered children at buffets.
- Some servers will let adults order off the children's menu.
- For an idea of how much food is likely to cost at the restaurants, as well as details on where to eat, check out our parks chapters.
- At **www.disneyland.disney.go.com/dining** you can check full sample restaurant menus before booking.
- Most restaurants have vegan and vegetarian options on the menu but speak to the chef if you have any specific requirements and they will do their best to accommodate you. Call ahead with a few days' notice if there is a particular place you want to eat to let them know you will be coming.
- If you have a food allergy, make this known when making your reservation and again to your server to b sure.
- Dining reservations are highly recommended for character meals.
- All restaurants, even the most expensive formal options, accommodate children with specially designed menus and facilities.
- Most people will eat at around the same time. To avoid long queues at counter service restaurants, avoid eating from midday to 2:00pm. The dinner rush is from 6:00pm to 9:00pm.
- Many dining locations in the theme parks and Downtown Disney stop serving food at 10:00pm even if the parks are open past this time. Ask for opening hours ahead of time if there is a specific place you want to dine.
- Some meals are advertised as "Mickey Check" meals on menus, these are Disney-approved nutritionally balanced meals designed for children.
- Feeling thirsty? If you want a cup of water, simply go to any Quick Service dining location and ask for an "ice water" at no cost. Or, refill water bottles at the water fountains dotted throughout the theme parks.
- If you bring drinks into the parks, which are allowed, be sure that they are not in glass bottles – these are not permitted in the theme parks. Neither are alcoholic drinks.

Quick Service Dining Recommendations:
- **Bengal Barbecue** – Adventureland, Disneyland Park. Serves meat and vegetable skewers.
- **Boardwalk Pizza & Pasta** – Paradise Pier, Disney California Adventure. Great flatbreads and pasta. Meatballs here contain cheese.
- **Cozy Cone Motel** – Cars Land, Disney California Adventure. Lots of different snacks.
- **Flo's V8 Café** – Cars Land, Disney California Adventure. Bigger portions than many other counter service restaurants. The kids' meal even comes served in a toy car that you can keep!

- **Harbour Galley** – Critter Country, Disneyland Park. The baked potatoes (stuffed with chicken, bacon or broccoli) are particularly nice.
- **Hungry Bear Restaurant** – Critter Country, Disneyland Park. Lots of variety.
- **Royal Street Veranda** – New Orleans Square, Disneyland Park. The clam chowder is a favorite of ours.
- **Pacific Wharf Café** – Pacific Wharf, Disney California Adventure. Serves soups and sandwiches.
- **Paradise Garden Grill** – Paradise Pier, Disney California Adventure. Meat and tofu skewers are the go to items here.
- **Village Haus** – Fantasyland, Disneyland Park. Serves flatbreads, burgers and sandwiches.

Full Service Dining Recommendations:
- **Carthay Circle**– Disney California Adventure. Great setting.
- **Napa Rose** – Grand Californian Hotel. Pricey fine dining at its best.
- **Wine Country Trattoria** – Disney California Adventure. The pasta dishes are great. Nice, relaxed atmosphere.

Character Dining:
If you want a guaranteed way to meet the characters with no queue lines, then look no further than character dining. This is where you will be able to have a meal, several Disney characters will visit each and every table for a chat, photos, signatures and more fun. Admittedly character dining experiences can be expensive but if characters are big in your book and you do not want to wait in line, character dining may be perfect for you.

Plaza Inn on Main Street, U.S.A. features characters until 11:00am at breakfast, as does Storyteller's Café at the Grand Floridian Hotel. At Goofy's Kitchen in the Disneyland Hotel and Disney's PCH Grill at Parade Pier Hotel you will find characters at both breakfast and dinner. Finally, at Ariel's Grotto in Disney California Adventure Park you can meet Ariel and her friends during lunch and breakfast. Ariel will be accompanied by two other Disney princesses (these can be either Snow White, Cinderella, Aurora or Belle).

Make sure to double check that characters will be present at your meal when reserving and again when entering a restaurant to avoid disappointment. A more detailed look at character dining can be seen in the "**Meeting the Characters**" chapter.

Chapter 15

Useful to Know:

Tips for Touring:

- **Wear comfortable shoes** – You will be walking miles and miles every day in the sun and in crowded conditions; therefore, comfortable shoes are a must. Make sure you break these in before going to the theme parks by wearing them for a week or two beforehand. Socks are also a must. Alternatively, flip-flops can be a good for when it rains but the weather is warm, as your feet will dry quickly.

- **Rent a stroller** – Do not underestimate needing to rent strollers for children who usually walk everywhere, as they will likely get tired after hours of walking. If you do not rent one, be prepared to do a lot of carrying. Many parents with children even up to the age of 8 rent strollers. They also give you a place to store bags, food and other belongings.

- **Get some rest** – Rest is important both during the day and at night. During the day we highly recommend you return to your hotel for a break, go to your room for a nap or have a swim in the pool and then return to the parks. We recommend you do this during the early afternoon straight after lunch (around midday to 4:00pm), as the parks will also be at their busiest during this time.

- **It is not Floridian Weather** – Unlike Florida, where in the summer you can expect to wear shorts and a tank top at 11:00pm while watching the fireworks and still feel warm, this is not the case in California. As it gets dark, the temperature drops drastically. We recommend you bring a sweater, hoody or light jacket for evenings in the theme parks.

- **Stay protected** – California is notorious for its heat and unrelenting sunshine. Take sunscreen and sunglasses and use them.

- **Check the weather** – It can get reasonably cold during some parts of the year, so be sure to check the weather forecast before leaving for your vacation, as well as before leaving for the parks each day.

- **When it rains** – If it rains, stay in the park as crowds will disperse; the park will be a lot less crowded and ride wait times will be shorter. Be aware that some attractions close during rain and shortly afterwards. Purchase a poncho or bring one from home, or carry a jacket.

- **Disposable cameras** – These may seem old-fashioned but if you visit your nearest store you can usually find these available for next to nothing. Give these to every member of your family and see the creative photos you can get. Kids and teenagers, in particular, are likely to snap some unique shots that you may have missed.

Stroller rentals:

Strollers, also known as buggies or pushchairs, can be rented at the stroller rental location at the Disneyland Resort. This is located to the right hand side of the turnstiles of Disneyland Park in the main plaza before entering the theme park. A single stroller, recommended for children of 50lbs of less, is $15 per day. Two strollers can be rented for $25 per day. Disneyland Resort-rented strollers can be used inside the two theme parks and between them, but cannot leave the main plaza. They are also not permitted in the Downtown Disney area.

Important Note: You can also bring your own stroller from home. Note that if you drive in to the Disneyland Resort you will need to board a tram to reach the theme parks; in order to bring a stroller onto the tram it must be collapsible or you will need to walk the 1-mile route from the parking garage to the parks.

Cast Member Insight: Having worked in the parks, we understand how necessary strollers are. Guests walk miles and miles every day – most likely more than they do back home – and kids do get tired. When parking strollers, use the designed stroller parking areas. These are generally where all the other strollers are parked. If your stroller is not in a designed stroller parking area, Cast Members will move it. Even if a stroller is parked in the correct area, it will still likely be shuffled by Cast Members to organize the layout better.

Do not just assume that a stroller has been taken because it is not where you left it; look around the area for it first. Also, do not use bike locks to attach your stroller to poles or railings – these are a fire hazard and your stroller may be removed by security.

Inevitably some strollers disappear, either by mistake or malice. Simply approach a Cast Member and let them know. You should be offered a complimentary Disney stroller to use throughout the day whether it is a personal stroller or a Disney stroller that has gone missing. You will also be given further instructions by the Cast Member.

Early Entry Options:

There are two early entry options at Disneyland Resort; the 'Early Entry' benefit can be used by any guest, whereas the 'Extra Magic Hours' benefit is exclusive to Disneyland Resort hotel guests.

Early Entry (Magic Mornings):

If you purchase a 3-day or longer ticket in advance it will include a "Magic Morning" admission which allows you to enter Disneyland Park one hour before the general public are allowed in – you get one Magic Morning per ticket. You can use the Magic Morning on Tuesdays, Thursdays or Saturdays. Guests with a 2016 Southern California CityPass can also take advantage of this offer.

Extra Magic Hours:

Guests staying at any of the on-site Disney hotels (Grand Californian Hotel, Disneyland Hotel and Paradise Pier Hotel) can enter one of the theme parks one hour before the general public. Extra Magic Hours at Disneyland Park are Tuesdays, Thursdays and Saturdays, and at Disney California Adventure are on Sundays, Mondays, Wednesdays and Fridays. Each guest must have an active room and valid park admission to take advantage of this early entry.

During Early Entry and Extra Magic Hours, only select attractions, shops and restaurants are open. In Disneyland, you will find select attractions open in Fantasyland and Tomorrowland. At Disney California Adventure you will find Cars Land open and select attractions in other lands.

Rider Switch:

The Rider Switch system allows adults to take turns riding an attraction, so that one can stay with a child while the other rides. The system means that they only need to queue up once for each attraction.

To use the system, simply go up to a Cast Member at an attraction entrance and ask to use Rider Switch. One adult will go through the normal queue line and another will be told how to get to the waiting area that is usually located near the ride exit. Once the first adult has ridden, they simply hand the child to the second adult who goes onto the ride immediately without waiting in line again. Rider Switch can also be used for groups of three or more where one person needs to stay with another who has a disability.

Rider Switch is available at: Autopia, Big Thunder Mountain Railroad, Gadget's Go Coaster, Indiana Jones Adventure, Matterhorn Bobsleds, Space Mountain, Splash Mountain, Star Tours: The Adventures Continue, California Screamin', Goofy's Sky School, Grizzly River Run, Radiator Springs Racers, Luigi's Rollickin' Roadsters, Silly Symphony Swings, Soarin' Over California, The Twilight Zone: Tower of Terror, and Tuck and Roll's Drive 'Em Buggies.

Height Restrictions:

For the safety of all guests, certain attractions at the Disneyland Resort have a minimum height requirement. This is strictly enforced at all attractions. It is worth measuring your children before visiting the resort to be aware of attractions they can and cannot do and to avoid disappointment. There are no exceptions to the height requirements at all. The following are the minimum height requirements at both theme parks:

32" (81 cm) or taller and accompanied by another rider 54" (137cm) or taller
- Autopia
- Mater's Junkyard Jamboree
- Luigi's Rollickin' Roadsters

35" (89 cm) or taller
- Gadget's Go Coaster

36" (91 cm) or taller
- Tuck and Roll's Drive' Em Buggies

40" (102 cm) or taller
- Big Thunder Mountain Railroad
- Jumpin' Jellyfish
- Radiator Springs Racers
- Silly Symphony Swings (tandem swings only)
- Soarin' Over California
- Space Mountain
- Splash Mountain
- Star Tours
- The Twilight Zone: Tower of Terror

42" (107 cm) or taller
- Goofy's Sky School
- Grizzly River Run
- Matterhorn Bobsleds
- Redwood Creek Challenge Trail (rock wall and zip line)

46" (117 cm) or taller
- Indiana Jones Adventure

48" (122 cm) or taller
- California Screamin'
- Silly Symphony Swings (to ride in a single swing)

54" (137 cm) or taller to ride alone
- Autopia

Free souvenirs:

There are a variety of souvenirs you can take home from your visit that you can get for free in the parks. Yes, you have paid admission to get inside but here are some extras that you can get at no extra cost to you. Many of these are not very well known!

- **Park Maps** – These are always a nice way to look back at your trip and are available throughout the parks. The times guide for Disneyland Park is also a neat listing of entertainment you may have seen.
- **Buena Vista Newspaper** – This is a great way of presenting the Disney California Adventure (DCA) park times guide in the form of a newspaper. It is a really nice souvenir, which is available on Buena Vista Street in DCA.
- **Celebration pins** – There are several different pins available from City Hall and Guest Services such as Happy Birthday, First Visit, Just Engaged or Happy Anniversary. Wear them around the parks to get special attention.
- **Honorary Citizen pin** – This is another pin you can get, but you have to earn this one. Visit City Hall and answer a question or two correctly about the Disney Universe to become an honorary citizen of Disneyland.
- **Driving license** from Autopia – Simply go through the queue line and ride the attraction; you will be given a license before you board.
- **Character Drawing** – Go to the Animation Academy and learn to draw one of many popular Disney characters. Then take your creative efforts home.
- **Restaurant menus** – Ask for a take-away menu and restaurants often have these pre-made.
- **Fastpasses** – If Disneyland is anything like the Walt Disney World Resort you can count on paper Fastpasses eventually disappearing. For now, though, grab these great mementos. Of course you will need to not use the Fastpasses to be able to keep them as souvenirs.
- **Dole Whip recipe cards** – Get these from the Tiki Juice Bar.
- **Jungle Cruise Maps and Haunted Mansion death certificates** – Ask at the end of the ride for these. They are not always available.
- **Mark Twain certificates for captains** – Ask to captain the ship and you will get a great view, plus a certificate at the end!
- **Lilly Belle ticket** – If you can get a ride on the iconic Lilly Belle train carriage (something which is very difficult to do), you can get a train ticket saying you have ridden in it. To get a ride, try being the first at the Main Street USA station in the morning before the park's opening

announcement is played and ask a Cast Member if they are taking reservations. There is no charge to ride the Lilly Belle.

- **Free LEGO** – The Downtown Disney LEGO store offers mini models for free once a month! You can see the dates of the LEGO Store Monthly Mini Model Build at **http://stores.lego.com/en-us/stores/us/orlando/**.

Cheap souvenirs:

- Antenna toppers
- Disney Dollars
- Pressed pennies
- Postcards
- Key chains
- Pens and pencils
- Magnets
- Silhouettes – From the Silhouette shop on Main Street USA
- Reusable tote bags
- Disney character dangles

Lost Children:

Disneyland teaches its Cast Members that there is no such thing as a lost child, only a lost adult, as Disneyland is a place made for children so they can never be lost. Nevertheless, this motto is unlikely to reassure parents too much. Fear not – having been in the industry for over 60 years, the Disneyland Resort is well equipped to deal with the issue.

If a Disneyland Cast Member finds an unattended child, they follow this procedure: the Cast Member will search around the area for a few minutes looking for the parent or guardian while comforting the child and trying to get as much useful information out of them as possible.

Then, if unsuccessful, they will take them to the Baby Care Center at each park – in Disneyland Park this is on the hub end of Main Street, U.S.A., and at Disney California Adventure this is located in the Pacific Wharf area. Lost children in the Downtown Disney district are taken either to the Disneyland Hotel or the Baby Care Center in Disneyland Park.

As a parent you should go to Guest Relations who hold a log of lost children, or alternatively go directly to the Baby Care Center at each park.

Other more thorough procedures are available for emergencies and you should contact Guest Relations for this information – there is a facility to page Team Leaders and Cast Members with a radio to the presence of a missing child.

In order to prevent or minimize the chance of a lost children, there are several key things you should do:

- Give your own child a nametag – inside a shirt, on a bracelet or elsewhere have a message saying "Hi I am [insert child's name here]. In the event of an emergency please contact" followed by your phone number. If they have an autograph book, the inner page of it is perfect for leaving your contact details.

- Never let go of your child's hand go if you usually hold it. Everything is very appealing to kids at Disneyland, and a child can be with you one second, and be gone the next. Even if you do not usually hold your child's hand, we recommend you do so in the parks – there are tens of thousands of other people and permanent physical contact will ensure you know exactly where your child is at all times.

- If you think you have lost your child, look around the immediate area thoroughly and call their name – children can find many spots to hideaway in.

- If your child is old enough to understand, teach them about Cast Members and their nametags – tell them to look out for someone with a nametag and to ask them for help if they are separated from you.

- Take a photo of your child in the morning so you have a reference point and can show Cast Members exactly what they are wearing and look like.

- For children who are old enough to roam the park, we recommend they each have a cell phone on them. Also, agree a meeting place and time within the park – you may want to do this two or three times throughout the day just to check that everything is all right with them.

- If you are allowing your child or children to ride an attraction or see a show on their own, be sure you know exactly where the exit is – ride exits are not always located by the entrance. Ask a Cast Member if you are unsure.

Guided Tours

If you want to experience the theme parks in a unique way, consider taking one of the guided tours on offer at the Disneyland Resort. These explore the history of the parks, tell you insider secrets and some even travel backstage into Cast Member only areas. Reservations can be made by calling 714-781-TOUR (8687) in advance.

There are several guided tours on offer:

- **Cultivating the Magic Tour** – Discover how important plants and foliage are in creating the themed environment at Disneyland Park. You will even tour select attractions with a focus on how the flora helps tell the story. Price: $49 per person. Duration: 2 hours.
- **Discover the Magic Tour** – In this tour you will be searching popular attractions for hints, you will solve puzzles and then receive a sweet treat at the end. This is more of a kids-focused tour with Disney character interaction included. Price: $59 per person. Duration: 2.5 hours.
- **Disney's Happiest Haunts Tour** – Join your "Ghost Host" for a night of happy haunts and spooky sightings throughout both theme parks. You will experience thrilling attractions and spine-tingling tales and enjoy a special Halloween treat. There is an optional "Ultimate Experience" package that allows you entry into the after-hours Mickey's Halloween Party. This tour is only offered during the Halloween season, usually mid-September to the end of October. Price: $85 per person. Duration: 2.5 hours.
- **"Walk in Walt's Disneyland Footsteps" Guided Tour** – In this unique experience you will get to learn about how and why Walt Disney built Disneyland, you will learn about his life, get to visit two classic attractions which debuted in 1955, and end with a meal on Main Street, U.S.A. Price: $109 per person. Duration: 3.5 hours.
- **Welcome to Disneyland Resort Tour** – Designed for first time visitors, this tour will teach you fun trivia as well as provide an overview of both theme parks at the Disneyland Resort. You will learn how to get premium spots for popular shows, make dining reservations and use Fastpass too. Price: $25 per person. Duration: 2.5 hours.
- **"Holiday Time at Disneyland" Tour** – Learn about how Disney's Holiday traditions started, how they have evolved over the years and hear enchanting Holiday tales. Experience attractions that have been specially spruced up for the Holiday season too! You will also get reserved parade viewing and delight in a tasty treat and a warm beverage. This tour is offered exclusively during the holiday season usually from mid-November to early January. Price: $85 per adult. Duration: 2.5 hours.

- **Disney California Story Tour** – Discover the story behind icons, attractions and landmarks as you experience California, much like Walt Disney once did! Set within Disney California Adventure Park, this trip back in time begins by giving you an intimate look into the members-only 1901 Lounge, before moving on to 3 of the park's most timeless, innovative and interactive attractions. As the tour reaches its conclusion, you are invited to top off your experience with a delicious lunch on Buena Vista Street—specially created just for tour participants! Price: $109 per person. Duration: 3 hours

Admission into the theme parks is required for all tours; this is not included in your tour price. Tours can be booked up to 30 days in advance. Same day bookings are sometimes available based on availability. Annual Passholders receive a 20% discount on all Disneyland Resort Guided Tours. Each of the Disneyland Resort Tours offers exclusive tour-specific collectables, such as pins, buttons and lanyards.

To pick up tickets for your tour proceed to the Disneyland Tour Gardens kiosk to the left of City Hall and check in for your tour at least 15 minutes before it begins. Then wait by the sign that says "Guided Tour Guests – Please Meet Your Tour Guide Here".

For the "Disney California Story Tour", check in at Chamber of Commerce in Disney California Adventure Park at least 15 minutes before it begins. Then wait by the sign that says "Guided Tour Guests – Please Meet Your Tour Guide Here".

VIP Guided Tour Services – These are private tours through the theme parks where you follow your own custom designed itinerary, and are the ultimate way to experience the Disneyland Resort if you can afford the price. Guests have full control over the duration and start time of their VIP Guided Tour. Party sizes can range from 1 guest to groups of 10.

Your tour will include: VIP viewing or seating for parades, select stage shows and nighttime spectaculars, and expedited entry to Fastpass attractions and a limited number of other attractions.

There is a minimum requirement of 6 hours per tour – pricing is $400 to $550 per Guide per hour depending on the season. Reservations can be made by calling 714-300-7710 up to 90 days in advance, though at least 72 hours' notice is recommended.

When to visit:

Crowds at the Disneyland Resort vary greatly from season to season and even from day to day. The difference of a single day can save you hundreds of dollars in hotel prices, as well as hours in line. You will have to consider the American national holidays and all surrounding countries, the weather, school vacations, pricing and more.

Below is a guide to the **best times of the year** to visit Disneyland Resort, and the times of the year to avoid. These are based on both crowd levels and room prices – but remember these are estimates. Weeks are rated from 1 to 10, with 1 being the absolute best time of the year to visit (very low crowds and the cheapest prices) and 10 being the absolute worst (very high crowds and the most expensive prices).

Week commencing:
January 3, 2016 – Overall rating: 7
January 10, 2016 – Overall rating: 5
January 17, 2016 – Overall rating: 4
January 24, 2016 – Overall rating: 3
January 31, 2016 – Overall rating: 4
February 7, 2016 – Overall rating: 7
February 14, 2016 – Overall rating: 9
February 21, 2016 – Overall rating: 5
February 28, 2016 – Overall rating: 5
March 6, 2016 – Overall rating: 6
March 13, 2016 – Overall rating: 9
March 20, 2016 – Overall rating: 9
March 27, 2016 – Overall rating: 9
April 3, 2016 – Overall rating: 9
April 10, 2016 – Overall rating: 6
April 17, 2016 – Overall rating: 5
April 24, 2016 – Overall rating: 4
May 1, 2016 – Overall rating: 5
May 8, 2016 – Overall rating: 4
May 15, 2016 – Overall rating: 5
May 22, 2016 – Overall rating: 8
May 29, 2016 – Overall rating: 7
June 5, 2016 – Overall rating: 7
June 12, 2016 – Overall rating: 8
June 19, 2016 – Overall rating: 8
June 26, 2016 – Overall rating: 8
July 3, 2016 – Overall rating: 10
July 10, 2016 – Overall rating: 9

July 17, 2016 – Overall rating: 9
July 24, 2016 – Overall rating: 9
July 31, 2016 – Overall rating: 8
August 7, 2016 – Overall rating: 7
August 14, 2016 – Overall rating: 7
August 21, 2016 – Overall rating: 6
August 28, 2016 – Overall rating: 4
September 4, 2016 – Overall rating: 6
September 11, 2016 – Overall rating: 2
September 18, 2016 – Overall rating: 2
September 25, 2016 – Overall rating: 3
October 2, 2016 – Overall rating: 6
October 9, 2016 – Overall rating: 5
October 16, 2016 – Overall rating: 5
October 23, 2016 – Overall rating: 7
October 30, 2016 – Overall rating: 3
November 6, 2016 – Overall rating: 6
November 13, 2016 – Overall rating: 7
November 20, 2016 – Overall rating: 9
November 27, 2016 – Overall rating: 8
December 4, 2016 – Overall rating: 5
December 11, 2016 – Overall rating: 6
December 18, 2016 – Overall rating: 10
December 25, 2016 – Overall rating: 10

It is important to note that whatever time of year you go to visit the Disneyland Resort, you will have fun. It is, however, inevitable that the less busy the parks are, the better it is for you as a guest – waiting times for attractions will be shorter and you will not have to deal with the scrum around the Resort's small pathways.

Disneyland's main clientele is comprised of locals – people who visit the parks regularly, and people with annual passes. As such, visitor patterns are different to other major theme park resorts such as Walt Disney World Resort which is filled with guests on vacation.

This makes it is relatively easy to predict weekly crowds at the parks. Saturdays are by far the busiest day of the week with locals swarming to the parks, this is closely followed by Sunday. Next it is Monday and Friday, Tuesday, Wednesday and finally Thursday is generally the least crowded day of all.

Of course, some exceptions to these rules may apply, mainly to do with national holidays and other celebrations. Specific days within these weeks may be much busier than others. For example, February 15th 2016 will be significantly busier than February 17th 2016, due to the former being on a Monday and the day after Valentine's Day.

Single Rider Lines:

One of the best ways to significantly reduce your time waiting in queue lines is to use the Single Rider line instead of the regular queue line. This is a completely separate queue line that is used to fill free spaces on ride vehicles. For example, if a ride vehicle can seat 8 people and a group of 4 turns up, followed by a group of 3, there is an empty space. Someone from the Single Rider queue line will fill that empty space.

Some rides do not have an obviously signposted Single Rider line: in this case simply ask the first attractions Cast Member you see (usually at the entrance to the attraction) whether they have a Single Rider line. They will direct you accordingly.

If there is a group of you, you can still use the Single Rider line, just be aware that you will not ride with each other but you can still meet at the exit of the ride. Single Rider Lines can be a huge timesaving service. Occasionally, the wait in a Single Rider line may exceed the regular wait time.

Single Rider lines are available at the following attractions. There are eight in total: *Splash Mountain, Matterhorn Bobsleds* and *Indiana Jones Adventure* at Disneyland Park, and *California Screamin', Goofy's Sky School, Grizzly River Run, Radiator Springs Racers* and *Soarin' Over California* at DCA.

Disneyland App

The Disneyland Resort smartphone app, simply called "Disneyland" is available on Apple and Android devices to enhance your vacation.

This app contains valuable information such as attraction wait times, character meet and greet locations, dining locations, restroom locations, PhotoPass locations, entertainment show schedules, and more on an interactive map that is updated in real time. Undoubtedly, the most useful feature of the app is the attraction wait times.

Guests can also purchase tickets directly via the app, and then show the ticket barcode on their mobile device to enter the parks

On-ride photos:

Many of Disney's rides have cameras positioned to take perfectly framed photos of you during the ride that would be impossible to take with your own handheld camera. You can get this photo after you have exited the ride.

What many people do not know, however, is that you do not have to buy on-ride photos straight after your ride; you can pick them up at any time during the day the photo was taken. Just remember your unique number at the attraction exit or ask a Cast Member to write it down for you.

If you like the photo, Cast Members will show it to you close up before you have to pay for it. If you like it, buy it! It is one of those memories you will really savor. Photo prices are $22 for two 5x7 prints and $19 for one 8x10 print. A digital download is available for $15.

Photopass:

Throughout the theme parks you will find Photopass photographers to take your photo in front of landmarks, at character meets and other experiences.

The photo products in this section work through a special Photopass card. You are given this card, at no cost to you, the first time you have a Photopass photo taken. You then use this Photopass card every time you take photos, handing it to the photographer for them to scan. Once your trip is over, enter the unique code printed on your Photopass card into the Photopass website and you will be able to see all your photos.

From there you can order a CD with all your photos, order individual prints or order digital download versions of the photos. You have 30 days to claim your photos on the website starting from the day the first photo is taken.

Individual prints are expensive, at around $15 each, so you may want to consider purchasing the Photopass CD which includes all in-park photos for $99.95 (plus taxes and shipping). Ride photos are not included.

Top Tip 1: Take a photo of your Photopass card and its barcode – that way if you lose the card you still have access to all the photos on it.
Top Tip 2: You can have multiple Photopass cards and add them all to one online account; make sure to add them at the same time to the same account.
Top Tip 3: Pre-order a PhotoPass+ package online at **www.disneyphotopass.com/specialoffers/dlrlearnmore.htm** for just $69.95 if booked more than 14 days before your vacation – this includes in-park photos, dining photos and attraction photos. A great value!

Where can I find this or that?

The Disneyland Resort is large and sometimes finding things is not as obvious as it may first seem. Here we have a list of common things that guests ask for, and where you can find them.

- **A phone charger** – At the Market House on Main Street USA, special charging lockers are available at the price of $2 per hour and include common charging cables. You can also plug in to any outlet (unless stated otherwise) throughout the parks if you have your charger with you, as long as you do not cause an obstruction to other guests. The *Great Moments with Mr. Lincoln* attraction is a good place to do this due to the low foot traffic and good availability of charging points.
- **Aspirin and other similar items** – At the Emporium shop on Main Street USA in Disneyland Park and Elias and Co. shop in DCA. You will need to ask a Cast Member as these items are kept behind the counter.
- **Batteries/Memory Cards/Disposable Cameras** – At most shops throughout both parks. Ask a Cast Member if you cannot find these.
- **Cash** – ATMs are throughout both parks and Downtown Disney.
- **Cigarettes** – Not sold throughout the entire Disneyland Resort property. The same applies to chewing gum.
- **Currency exchange** – At City Hall in Disneyland Park, and Guest Relations in DCA.
- **Kennels** – At the parking location at 1313 Harbor Blvd. These are priced at $20 per day per animal. Many animals are accepted. Food is provided for the animals at no extra charge if you request this. Proof of vaccines is required. More information is available by calling 714-781-4565 ahead of your visit.
- **Lockers** – Inside and outside both theme parks.
- **Lost and Found** – When standing outside Disneyland Park facing the turnstiles walk to the buildings on the left. Here you will find Lost and Found for the entire resort.
- **Lost Children** – At the Baby Care Center on the hub-side of Main Street in Disneyland Park, and in the Pacific Wharf area of DCA.
- **Lost Adults** – At City Hall in Disneyland Park and Guest Relations in DCA. Messages can also be left here for lost parents/adults.
- **Package Storage** – If it is a Disney-bought item, you can have it delivered to Package Pickup at both parks simply by asking at the time of purchase. On-site hotel guests can have packages delivered to their hotel.
- **Ponchos/Rainwear** – Available at every shop for purchase. You may need to ask a Cast Member, as these may be behind the counter.
- **Sunscreen/Sunblock** – At the Emporium shop on Main Street

USA in Disneyland Park and Elias and Co. shop in DCA. You will need to ask a Cast Member as these items are kept behind the counter.

Not to be missed – The best of each park:

Your time at the Disneyland Resort is limited. So, to help you make the most of your visit, we have compiled a list of our favorite rides, shows and attractions for each park. These rides have been chosen because of their storytelling abilities, for being Disneyland classics, their technological superiority, their thrills, how fun they are, or a combination of all the above.

Next to each ride we have noted our reasoning for choosing them. We feel that by experiencing the attractions listed below you will get unique experiences only offered at a Disney park.

Disneyland Park:

Adventureland:
- Jungle Cruise – Theming, Disney classic
- Indiana Jones Adventure – Technology, Thrill, Theming

Fantasyland:
- it's a small world – Disney classic
- Peter Pan's Flight – Disney classic
- Matterhorn Bobsleds – Thrill

Tomorrowland:
- Buzz Lightyear Astro Blasters – Fun
- Space Mountain – Thrill
- Star Tours: The Adventures Continue – Theming, Thrill, and Technology

Mickey's Toontown:
- Roger Rabbit's Car Toon Spin – Fun

Frontierland:
- Big Thunder Mountain – Thrill, Theming, Storytelling

New Orleans Square:
- Haunted Mansion – Theming, Storytelling, Disney Classic
- Pirates of the Caribbean – Theming, Storytelling, Small Thrill, Disney Classic

Critter Country:
- Splash Mountain – Theming, Storytelling, Thrill
- The Many Adventure of Winnie the Pooh – Storytelling

Entertainment:
- Soundsational (Parade)
- Paint the Night (Parade)
- Mickey and the Magical Map (Show)
- Fireworks
- Fantasmic (Nighttime Show)

Disney California Adventure

Hollywood Land:

- Animation Academy – Disney Classic, Fun
- The Twilight Zone: Tower of Terror – Thrill, Theming, Storytelling,
- Monsters, Inc. Mike & Sulley to the Rescue! – Fun, Theming, Storytelling

Paradise Pier:

- California Screamin' – Thrill
- Goofy's Sky School – Thrill
- The Little Mermaid: Ariel's Undersea Adventure – Disney Classic, Storytelling
- Toy Story Midway Mania – Fun, Technology
- Turtle Talk with Crush – Storytelling, Technology

Grizzly Peak:

- Grizzly River Run – Thrill, Fun, Theming

Cars Land:

- Radiator Springs Racers – Thrill, Fun, Theming, Storytelling

Condor Flats:

- Soarin' Over California – Thrill, Storytelling

Entertainment:

- Pixar Play Parade
- World of Color (Nighttime Show)

Chapter 16
How to spend less time queuing

The Disneyland Resort meticulously themes its queues to immerse you into the atmosphere and to begin to tell the story of the ride you are about to get on before you step foot on it. However, sometimes you just want to forget queuing and get on the rides as quickly as possible. If you do not set out with a strategy, then you WILL spend longer in queues than you need to.

Here are our top tips on minimizing your wait times:

- **Disney hotel guests** – If you are staying at a Disneyland resort hotel take advantage of the Extra Magic Hours benefit. This gets you entry into Disneyland Resort's theme parks one whole hour before regular park guests do. This benefit is available every day of the week. Only one of the parks is open early each day. So, if the regular park opening time is 9:00am, you will be able to enter from 8:00am onwards. During very busy periods both parks may open early. We recommend you be at the park entrances 20 to 30 minutes before this time.
  - o Early entry for Disneyland Park is on Tuesday, Thursday and Saturday. Early entry for California Adventure is Sunday, Monday, Wednesday and Friday.
  - o At Disneyland Park, Fantasyland and Tomorrowland are open – as well as select attractions in each land. These vary from day to day but usually include: Alice in Wonderland, Buzz Lightyear Astro Blasters, Dumbo the Flying Elephant, Fantasy Faire, Finding Nemo Submarine Voyage, King Arthur Carrousel, Mad Tea Party, Matterhorn Bobsleds, Mr. Toad's Wild Ride, Monorail, Peter Pan's Flight, Pinocchio's Daring Journey, Snow White's Scary Adventures, Space Mountain and Star Tours. Shops and dining locations on Main Street will also be open.
  - o At California Adventure, attractions will be open in several of the lands including Cars Land. Attractions that are typically open include: California Screamin', Mater's Junkyard Jamboree, Luigi's Rollickin' Roadsters, Radiator Springs Racers, Soarin' Over California, The Little Mermaid: Ariel's Undersea Adventure, The Twilight Zone: Tower of Terror and Toy Story Midway Mania. We recommend you go straight to Radiator Springs Racers during this time if the wait is under 30 minutes. Alternatively, you should use the time to do all the other big attractions – most of which will have no line at all! World of Color Fastpasses are also distributed during this time. No other Fastpass machines operate until park opening. Lines at the main park turnstiles are

usually much shorter than lines at thr Grand Californian Hotel turnstiles during this Extra Magic Hour period.

- **Early entry for multi-day ticket holders** – If you purchase a 3-day, or longer, ticket in advance you will get one Magic Morning admission to Disneyland Park. Select Fantasyland and Tomorrowland attractions are open during this time. Note: This Magic Morning can be used only one time during your stay for Disneyland Park only, not California Adventure.

- **The theme parks open early** – Disneyland Park's opening hours usually state it opens at 9:00am, but any guest can enter the park half an hour earlier. This means you can start to go in and take photos of Main Street, U.S.A., start shopping, eating and enjoy the atmosphere.

At the end of Main Street, U.S.A. just before you come to the hub in front of the castle, the area will be cordoned off by Cast Members (if you are a Disney hotel guest and have a Magic Morning admission, you can enter Fantasyland and Tomorrowland as mentioned above). Otherwise wait by the rope for "rope-drop" – this is when the speakers blare a fanfare and you are told, "Disneyland Park is now open!" You will be reminded to "walk to your first destination".

Be there for park opening and you can get on your first ride in minutes. At Disney California Adventure, the park also opens about 30 minutes early and you can start getting in line for Radiator Springs Racers Fastpasses from this time, and explore Buena Vista Street. The line for Radiator Springs Racers Fastpasses can be very, very long but Fastpasses are often gone within 2 hours of the park opening, so it is your only chance to get them.

- **Beware of Frozen** – When *Frozen: Live at the Hyperion* is playing, wait times for the surrounding attractions (*Tower of Terror* and *Monsters Inc.*) are typically lower than at other times. Try to avoid the area just after a show has finished as thousands of guests leave the show looking for more attractions, which means longer wait times at surrounding rides and shows. The exodus of people occurs about 40 minutes after the scheduled start of each show.

- **The Fantasmic and Fireworks secret** – In the evenings, crowds are drawn to Frontierland for Fantasmic, and Main Street, U.S.A. for the fireworks and the Paint the Night Parade. That means that the other lands are much less crowded – Tomorrowland, in particular!

- **Post-firework riding** – Check what time Disneyland Park's firework show is being performed, as well as Paint the Night, Fantasmic, and World of Color. If the park remains open after the fireworks, which it regularly does, then you can keep riding the attractions until the park closes. On any day, as long as you are in the queue before the park officially closes you will be able to ride. By this time of the night, however, queues should be minimal or non-existent. You should be able to walk on to most rides. A huge number of guests leave after the fireworks to go back to their hotel or home to sleep.

• **Ride outdoor attractions during the rain** – Outdoor rides have significantly shorter queues when it is raining. Yes, you may get soaked but you will queue for a shorter time too! Note that some attractions do not operate in the rain.

• **See our section on the less busy times** – If you are visiting on New Year's Day expect to queue a lot longer than in the middle of September. If you are going on a weekend, expect to wait longer than on a weekday. See our section on when to visit to avoid the biggest crowds.

• **Go shopping at the start or end of the day** – If you have come in early, why not go shopping for a bit before the park officially opens? Alternatively, go shopping at the end of the day; even when the park is "officially" closed, the shops on Main Street, U.S.A. stay open for one hour longer "for your shopping convenience". Or, just walk over to Downtown Disney and go shopping there! Alternatively, Disney hotels have a small store inside them too. Do not waste time during the day shopping.

• **Pick up your guide to the parks on the way in** – Get your park map and the Times Guide on the way into the parks, at your hotel or at the turnstiles. It means you will not miss parades, shows, fireworks, and meet and greet times and locations.

Chapter 17

Comparing the Disneyland Resort and the Walt Disney World Resort

Although the Disneyland Resort opened in 1955 to great success, Walt Disney wanted something bigger. However, his dream of the Florida Project, or Disney World, was never realized before his death. In honor of his lifelong work, the company decided to call the resort *Walt* Disney World after the company's founder.

Based just outside Orlando, Florida the resort is over 40 square miles in size. Compared to the Disneyland Resort, Walt Disney World Resort encompasses almost ten times as many hotels, twice as many theme parks, two water parks, golf courses and more. It is significantly bigger than the Disneyland Resort and offers tons of extra activities. Size is not everything though, and the two resorts both have their upsides and downsides. Discover them all here.

The atmosphere:
Walt Disney World is the largest resort and naturally the atmosphere varies from place to place and park to park – but ultimately due to its size and the amount of time it takes to get off-property, the resort is very good at keeping you in the "Disney bubble" and within the Disney magic. Everywhere you go you will see Mickey-shaped road signs, perfectly shaped lawns and Disney characters. It truly is an immersive atmosphere. Walt Disney World's Magic Kingdom does not have the charm of the Disneyland Resort though, seeming more "fake" and oversized.

Disneyland Resort has a much quainter atmosphere to it with everything being very small compared to its Floridian friend, but we instantly liked it more than the Walt Disney World Resort. However, attractions in the parks can be almost too close together, with walkways getting very easily crowded. Disneyland Resort is also the opposite of Walt Disney World – at Disneyland it is very easy to leave the atmosphere behind and step into the real world. At Disneyland you can simply walk off property in a couple of minutes. Whether that is a positive or negative point is up to you.

Offerings:
Walt Disney World has the widest offering, with four theme parks. Magic Kingdom Park, Epcot, Hollywood Studios and Animal Kingdom containing some incredible unique attractions and themed environments, as well as some Disneyland Resort clones.

Where else can you have a safari ride on *Kilimanjaro Safaris*, then get a bus to Epcot and fly around the world in *Soarin'*, take a boat to Hollywood Studios and drop 13-stories in the *Tower of Terror* and finally finish off your night by watching *Wishes* fireworks in front of Cinderella Castle?

The Walt Disney World Resort has a wealth of experiences to be explored including two water parks, golf courses, the countless resort hotels and the unique adventures you can take part in such as resort guided tours. Let's not forget the fact that you can go parasailing, take boats between resorts, go on carriage rides, sit on a beach, hire out a speedboat, visit Disney Springs and much more at the Walt Disney World Resort too! Walt Disney World hands down beats Disneyland Resort in terms of its offerings.

Disneyland Resort offers two theme parks with some incredible unique attractions such as *Radiator Springs Racers* and *Indiana Jones Adventure*. Outside the two theme parks, there is the decently sized (but smaller than Walt Disney World's) Downtown Disney area. There are no golf courses, no water parks, only three on-site Disney resort hotels and no unique experiences outside the parks.

Attractions:

Let's face it: most people go to theme parks for the attractions. You would not pay a park's daily admission price to go and eat in a restaurant, or walk around in a themed environment. Attractions are king.

Walt Disney World has a huge variety of attractions, although some are clones of others at the Disneyland Resort – and inferior versions at that, such as *it's a small world* and *Pirates of the Caribbean*. It does have many unique attractions though: *Expedition Everest, Mickey's Philharmagic*, interactive experiences, *Mission: SPACE, Ellen's Energy Adventure* and *Test Track*. It also has different versions of *Splash, Big Thunder* and *Space Mountain*.

The *World Showcase* in Epcot is composed of a multitude of incredible, immersive experiences – a true testament to Disney's quality of theming. However, we feel that Magic Kingdom Park lacks in old-style classic dark rides such as *Snow White,* though it is nice to see the *Carousel of Progress* still in operation. Hollywood Studios feels like it lacks rides in general, and is filled with shows to pad its offerings; this park is going through a massive overhaul at the moment to correct this.

Fastpass+ implementation, has not been done successfully in our opinion, with rides such as *Toy Story Midway Mania* and *Peter Pan's Flight* having huge standby queues at Walt Disney World because of the system. In general, lines are much more manageable at Disneyland. Our main issue with attractions at Walt Disney World is the lack of them – the parks need many more attractions to deal with the crowds they pull in on a daily basis.

Disneyland Resort has several very unique attractions such as *Matterhorn Bobsleds, Finding Nemo Submarine Voyage, Indiana Jones Adventure, California Screamin', Grizzly River Run, Alice in Wonderland, Mr. Toad's Wild Ride, Monster's Inc.: Mike and Sulley to the Rescue,* and *Radiator Springs Racers* to name but a few.

You can also actually go inside the castle at Disneyland and see it, unlike at Walt Disney World. Some attractions such as *it's a small world, Winnie the Pooh* and *Pirates of the Caribbean* are also better than their Floridian counterparts, though *Space Mountain* is comparatively a bit boring here in our opinion.

The lack of *Rock 'n' Rollercoaster* at the Disneyland Resort saddens us. Also, the water rides here really do get you wet unlike those in Florida. Overall, both parks feel like they have a good number of attractions to fill a few days, and there is no weaker park at the resort.

Accommodation:
Walt Disney World has the largest variety of resort hotels with more than can be counted on your hands. The 'deluxe' hotels, in particular, have a quality that make you forget you are in Central Florida by immersing you in a different environment – you can be taken to a campsite, to the wilderness, Polynesia, Africa, the Victorian Era, the world of Pixar, New Orleans and much more. The theming at the hotels is second to none, as are the amenities on offer. The range of prices is also very appealing.

Disneyland Resort – Only one of the hotels, the Grand Californian, really has the immersive quality at the Disneyland Resort that is so prevalent at Walt Disney World. The other on-site hotels seem like any other hotel with Disney branding overlaid, unfortunately. There are only three hotels too, and they are all *very* expensive. They seem even more expensive when you can get a non-Disney hotel with comparable amenities for a fraction of the price two minutes' walk away.

Resort size:
Walt Disney World – The resort is huge, spanning 47 square miles (twice the size of Manhattan). That means Disney has a lot of room to build things such as lakes, resort hotels and golf courses – the resort also still has enough free land to double in size. However, at times, the resort seems almost too big: things sometimes seem unnecessarily spaced out and when it takes 20 minutes on a bus to get from your hotel to the Magic Kingdom you know size can be a hindrance.

Disneyland Resort – This is a tiny resort with a very intimate feel, although Disneyland Park can feel a little small and cramped, in our opinion. Everything is within walking distance, including the two parks, which are literally opposite each other. Due to its location, Disneyland does not really have additional room for expansion.

Entertainment - Shows, Parades and Characters:
Walt Disney World – Magic Kingdom Park provides a wealth of entertainment, with dozens of character meet and greats. Unfortunately, there is only one real live 'stage show', which takes place in front of the castle. Magic Kingdom offers quite a few sit-down recorded shows such as *Mickey's Philharmagic, Monster's Inc., Stitch, Carousel of Progress, Hall of Presidents, Country Bear Jamboree* and *The Enchanted Tiki Room*; some are excellent but many feel vastly out of date. Animal Kingdom Park offers the most unique shows, followed by Disney's Hollywood Studios. Epcot's World Showcase is filled with streetmosphere (as is Hollywood Studios) and cinema-style shows too. Only Magic Kingdom Park offers a parade.

Nighttime entertainment is widespread throughout the parks, with each park having a nighttime show. In the evening, Epcot presents *Illuminations*, Magic Kingdom presents the wonderful *Main Street Electrical Parade, Celebrate the Magic* and *Wishes*, Hollywood Studios presents the magical *Fantasmic*, and Animal Kingdom presents *Rivers of Light*.

Characters can be found throughout the parks but not usually 'randomly', they are usually part of scheduled meet and greets. Furthermore, there are little touches that Magic Kingdom Park has such as the *Welcome Show* and the *Trolley Show* in the morning that are a magical start to the day, and the unadvertised *Kiss Goodnight* at the end of the day. These are truly unique experiences.

To improve the entertainment roster at Walt Disney World it needs more stage shows at Magic Kingdom Park, the addition of parades at the other parks, and more random character meet and greets.

Disneyland Resort has many more random character appearances, incredible casting with characters who are exceptionally true to life, four nighttime shows in just two parks and many, many more stage shows.

The parades at the two parks are also the most creative and fun parades we have ever seen too – 'Soundsational', 'Pixar Play Parade' and 'Paint the Night' beat anything Walt Disney World has to offer.

Plus, with luck and careful timing you can see several of the nighttime shows, across both parks, on the same night.

'Disneyland Forever' is a great firework show at Disneyland; it is very different to Walt Disney World's *'Wishes'* and we'd rate them equally.

Food:
Walt Disney World has the luxury of offering many different types of food, particularly throughout its resort hotels. You can go to Boma and get a taste of Africa, visit the countries in the World Showcase at Epcot and try Canadian and Italian food, or simply settle for simpler theme park fare. Prices are more expensive than comparable food outlets in the US, but are still reasonably priced as far as theme park food goes. Dining reservations start 180 days in advance and popular restaurants have to be booked as soon as reservations open to avoid missing out.

Disneyland Resort offers significantly fewer food options than the Walt Disney World Resort but has some great breakfast offerings, especially in Adventureland. The food at Disneyland Resort is more standard theme park fare (though there are some great dining experiences in the hotels and theme parks), and there are definitely fewer table service restaurants to eat in than at Walt Disney World. Dining reservations only open 60 days in advance, and getting these is much easier.

The Magic and the Cast Members:

The Cast Members at **Walt Disney World** are hugely empowered to create magic with tools such as vouchers to replace damaged or lost items. There are also planned magical moments throughout the day such as free cake by the teacups ride at the Magic Kingdom Park, free desserts at quick service locations and being able to pull the sword out of the stone by the carousel at Magic Kingdom Park – all done in a seemingly random fashion. Magic is everywhere and Cast Members are both empowered, and encouraged, to create it.

Disneyland Resort is very much like Walt Disney World. The Cast Members, however, do go above and beyond to make your day special, in our experience; they will do anything possible to make your visit unforgettable.

Miscellaneous:

Disneyland Resort – The whole park was clearly designed for standards of 60 years ago. For example, the turnstiles are tiny and accessibility is not as great either. Everything did, however, seem more relaxed and natural than at Walt Disney World. You get the same quality of service just without it feeling like it is being faked by the Cast Member. The cast at Disneyland Resort just seem to naturally enjoy their jobs more. The roping off of crowds during parades and fireworks is a great way to keep walkways clear – we were very impressed with this, and it is something that should be adopted at Walt Disney World. Sadly, there is no Wi-Fi in the parks.

Walt Disney World has Wi-Fi in the parks, which is a great addition. The weather being generally warm year-round is great, but hurricane season as well as the hot, humid summers can put a downer on things. Views on Fastpass+ vary but planning far, far in advance is almost compulsory.

Overall:

Disneyland Resort is the perfect resort for locals and vacationers alike and we can see why it has done so well. Even 60 years after opening it still captures a truly magical era, yet the resort is not afraid of keeping up with the times. For a resort that is a fraction of the size of Walt Disney World, Disneyland Resort is still world class: a testament to how this small theme park resort has kept up with the times.

Walt Disney World is truly what it says on the tin - a world of Disney - it can be almost inescapable once you are in its claws, but in a good way. You really do get immersed inside the Disney bubble, and it is easy to see why it is the world's most visited tourist destination.

Ride and attraction comparisons:

This section lists all the attractions at the Disneyland Resort and explains how they compare to their Walt Disney World Resort counterparts, as well as listing the ones that are completely original. The aim is that if you have been to the Walt Disney World Resort, you will not have to spend time repeating attractions, and can make the most your time at Disneyland Resort.

Attractions that are completely unique to the Disneyland Resort:

- Alice in Wonderland
- The Bakery Tour
- California Screamin'
- Captain EO (this no longer exists at Epcot)
- Casey Jr. Circus Train
- Character Close-Up
- Chip n Dale Treehouse
- Davy Crockett's Explorer Canoes
- The Disney Gallery
- Disneyland Monorail (like the transportation system in Walt Disney World, but this one here is an in-park attraction)
- The Disneyland Story presenting Great Moments with Mr. Lincoln (like the Hall of Presidents in Walt Disney World's Magic Kingdom, but a different show)
- Finding Nemo Submarine Voyage
- Flik's Flyers
- Francis' Ladybug Boogie
- Gadget's Go Coaster
- Golden Zephyr
- Goofy's Playhouse
- Goofy's Sky School
- Grizzly River Run (like Kali River Rapids but this is an entirely different and much better experience)
- Heimlich's Chew Chew Train
- Indiana Jones Adventure
- Jumpin' Jellyfish
- King Triton's Carousel
- Luigi's Rollickin' Roadsters
- Main Street Cinema
- Mater's Junkyard Jamboree
- Matterhorn Bobsleds
- Mickey's Fun Wheel
- Minnie's House
- Monsters, Inc. Mike & Sulley to the Rescue!
- Mr. Toad's Wild Ride
- Pinocchio's Daring Journey
- Radiator Springs Racers
- Red Car Trolley
- Redwood Creek Challenge Trail
- Roger Rabbit's Cartoon Spin
- Sailing Ship Columbia
- Silly Symphony Swings
- Sleeping Beauty Castle Walkthrough
- Snow White's Scary Adventures (this was previously at Walt Disney World but has now closed and been replaced)
- Sorcerer's Workshop
- Storybook Land Canal Boats
- Tarzan's Treehouse
- Tuck and Roll's Drive 'Em Buggies

Attractions that exist in Walt Disney World but have some differences:

- Astro Orbitor – The Disneyland version is on the ground and not high up in the air like at Walt Disney World.
- Autopia – Slightly different to WDW's version. This one is more scenic but a very similar experience overall.
- Big Thunder Mountain Railroad – Similar in style to the WDW version, but we prefer this version, especially after its recent refurbishment.
- Buzz Lightyear Astro Blasters – Similar to Walt Disney World but with different interior scenes and more interactive guns.
- Disneyland Railroad – More stops and grander than its Walt Disney World counterpart.
- Dumbo the Flying Elephant – We prefer the WDW version with its interactive queue for kids and lower wait times with two sets of Dumbos.
- "it's a small world" – Very similar but we prefer this version due to the inclusion of subtle Disney characters. The attraction also gets a cool holiday overlay here, which it does not in Florida.
- Jungle Cruise – There is a reordering of the scenes here and there is no indoor section like at Walt Disney World. It is largely the same experience though.
- Main Street Vehicles – Different vehicles are used here.
- Mickey's House and Meet Mickey – This exists at Walt Disney World but in a different format; the queue here is much more fun. However, Mickey talks in Walt Disney World so we prefer the Floridian version of this attraction.
- Peter Pan's Flight – Many scenes are identical between the two versions but the ride experience is very similar. This version also does not have Fastpass.
- Tom Sawyer Island – Completely different exploration area.
- Pirates of the Caribbean – Multiple drops and different scenes throughout in the Disneyland version. You also may get slightly splashed in this version. This version also does not have Fastpass.
- Space Mountain – Completely different ride layout and storyline, the Walt Disney World version has more drops and is more exciting, but the Disneyland version is arguably more elaborately themed. The Disneyland version also gets seasonal overlays.
- Splash Mountain – This ride is shorter at Disneyland but you get wetter here than at Walt Disney World. The storyline and the interiors are laid out differently, but they are very similar overall.
- The Twilight Zone: Tower of Terror – A very similar experience to

Florida but there is a different scene order and at Disneyland there is an absence of the horizontal elevator movement. This version is less prone to technical difficulties due to its different ride system.

Attractions that are clones of those at the Walt Disney World Resort:

- Animation Academy
- Enchanted Tiki Room
- Frontierland Shootin' Exposition
- Haunted Mansion (with the exception of the exterior and the one missing scene in the Disneyland version, the two attractions are clones). The attraction at the Disneyland Resort also gets a really cool Halloween and Christmas makeover in California.
- It's Tough to be a Bug!
- King Arthur Carrousel – Visually it is a different theme, but ride-wise it is very much the same
- The Little Mermaid: Ariel's Undersea Adventure – The queue line in WDW is much better but there is hardly ever a line to wait in at the Disneyland Resort, whereas wait times can top 45 minutes at Walt Disney World
- Mad Tea Party
- The Many Adventures of Winnie the Pooh – There is the addition of narration at Disneyland, plus there is rarely a wait. Walt Disney World's version has a better queue line.
- Mark Twain Riverboat
- Soarin' Over California – At the Disneyland Resort there is a different queue line but there is usually also a much shorter wait.
- Star Tours - The Adventures Continue
- Toy Story Midway Mania – The ride experience is the same but Disneyland Resort's version does not have Fastpass. The queue line is different too.
- Turtle Talk with Crush

Chapter 18

Seasonal Events

Throughout the year there is always something different happening at the Disneyland Resort – with everything from religious celebrations, to marathons, to after hours' parties, there is something for everyone. The main period where the entire resort is "standard" with no special events is during the busy summer period of late June through the end of August.

Season of the Force – November 16th 2015 onwards. No end date announced yet.

Traveling to a galaxy far, far away is easier than ever for guests visiting the Disneyland Resort. There are a variety of new experiences during this season:

• Star Wars Launch Bay – Meet iconic characters such as Darth Vader, Chewbacca or even Boba Fett; experience The Cantina from the movies; play current and upcoming Star Wars video games at the Game Center; find replicas of film props in both the Light Side and Dark Side galleries; and much more.

• Star Tours: The Adventures Continue – A new adventure awaits guests with scenes and characters from the Star Wars: The Force Awakens.

• Hyperspace Mountain – The popular Space Mountain attraction is reimagined as Hyperspace Mountain, thrusting guests into an X-wing Starfighter battle as they race through the darkness. The guest experience is enhanced by a new soundtrack, inspired by the films' musical themes and re-orchestrated to match every move in the attraction.

• Jedi Training: Trials of the Temple – This reimagined battle experience takes younglings to the secret site of an ancient Jedi temple, where they discover if they have the makings of a true Jedi. Villains such as Darth Vader and the Seventh Sister Inquisitor from the popular Disney XD series Star Wars Rebels join the adventure.

• Star Wars: Path of the Jedi – Guests can relive stories from the Star Wars saga, or discover them for the first time, through this short, film compilation at Tomorrowland Theater. It includes moments from the new film, Star Wars: The Force Awakens. This cinematic short connects iconic scenes from the films in fun new ways, following the journey of Luke Skywalker.

This new event began in 2015 for the first time and could well become a yearly event at the Disneyland Resort.

Holiday Season – November 13th 2015 to January 6th, 2016

Come and celebrate the jolliest season of them all at the happiest place on earth. The entirety of Disneyland Park is overrun with Christmas decorations including a huge Christmas tree to marvel at (with over 200 ornaments). The Haunted Mansion has a "Nightmare before Christmas" overlay until the end of the season, "it's a small world" gets a holiday themed interior and exterior, the Jungle Cruise gets a holiday makeover, Main Street, U.S.A. sees snow several times a day, there is a Christmas themed parade, there are seasonal shows, and you can meet characters in their Christmas best. Plus, you can expect seasonal treats abound.

Usually a special Holiday fireworks display is performed during this period but for 2015 this is not the case. 'Disneyland Forever', the special 60th anniversary firework spectacular, will be performed nightly instead.

On two dates during the holiday season (December 5th and 6th in 2015), you can also watch Disneyland's "Candlelight Processional", a spectacle with traditional Christmas songs and a retelling of the Christmas story by a celebrity narrator.

At Disney California Adventure, 'World of Color' takes on a Christmas twist with an entirely different show from the one that runs throughout the rest of the year. At least one performance of the seasonal 'World of Color – Winter Dreams' will be performed each night, as well as one of 'World of Color – Celebrate', the special show for the 60th anniversary celebration.

The "Disney ¡Viva Navidad!" party includes traditional Mexican food, music and fun activities. We can also guarantee that DCA will be full of Christmas ornaments everywhere, even in Cars Land.

The holiday season is especially busy, but particularly surrounding the week before and after Christmas Day itself. Be sure to be at the parks early, as they will fill to capacity and guests will not be allowed in once full.

Unlike at Walt Disney World, here all entertainment is included in your standard theme park admission and there are no after-hours extra-charged Holiday parties.

Top Tip: Have you ever seen the Disney Christmas Day Parade broadcast on ABC on Christmas Day? It's actually filmed several weeks in advance – at Disneyland filming usually takes place on the 1st or 2nd weekend of November. Park guests can experience this taping at no extra charge.

New Year Celebrations – December 31st 2015 to January 1st 2016
If you want to ring in the New Year in style, then this may be the event for you. Included in your regular park admission, you can mark the moment the year changes through an incredible firework display.

Note that New Year's Eve and New Year's Day are both incredibly popular events and the resort will be very, very busy. Parks will fill to capacity early in the day which means that after a certain time no more guests will be allowed inside the theme parks for safety reasons.

Wait times will be long for rides: Fastpasses are definitely needed but these will run out early in the day. In our opinion, despite the incredible feeling of community and warmth you get by sharing this event with so many others, it is not worth the hassle. Many however, would disagree with us!

Día de los Reyes Magos (**Three Kings Day**) – January 2nd to January 6th 2016
This is a traditional Mexican, Spanish and Central American celebration and celebrates the Magi bringing gifts to Jesus. The Disneyland Resort celebrates this in style with five days filled with festive fun with characters in themed costumes, specialty food items and unique entertainment.

Star Wars Half Marathon Weekend – January 14th to January 17th 2016
May the Force be with you during the *Star Wars* Half Marathon Weekend. It is a weekend journey to a galaxy far, far away featuring various runs, special events, Disney entertainment, your favorite *Star Wars* and Disney characters to cheer you along the course, and much, much more!

There is a run for Jedi Knights and Padawans of every age and skill level, including the *Star Wars* Half Marathon, *Star Wars* 10K and *Star Wars* 5K, and the *run*Disney Kid Races. Put yourself to the ultimate test and join the *Star Wars* Rebel Challenge combining the *Star Wars* 10K and Half Marathon for an out-of-this-world running adventure.

Mardi Gras – Selected dates from January to February each year. 2016 dates not yet available.
Celebrate the Carnival celebrations in style in the New Orleans Square area of Disneyland Park. You will find special entertainment from the likes of Princess Tiana and Prince Naveen, as well as the opportunity to meet other Disney characters like Mickey and Minnie in their Mardi Gras costumes.

Lunar New Year – Selected dates in February. 2016 dates not yet available.

This event, also known as Chinese New Year, is celebrated at the Disneyland Resort every year including special character appearances from the likes of Mulan and Mushu, as well as specialty food items and children's activities.

Easter – One month around Easter Sunday. Exact 2016 dates not yet announced.
Delight in some egg-celent fun by meeting classic Disney characters, as well as the Easter Bunny and other Disney rabbits. There is even a country band that performs several times a day. 2016 dates have not yet been announced.

Tinker Bell Half Marathon – May 5th to 8th 2016

This yearly half marathon takes place all across the Disneyland Resort with Disney characters and entertainment along the course. As well as the 13.1-mile Tinker Bell half marathon, you can also participate in the Tinker Bell 10K, Never Land Family Run 5K and the Kids Races. As well as this, there is an Expo and a 'Pasta in the Park' party.

Independence Day – July 4th

Every year you can celebrate the Independence of the USA with an evening of American celebration at the Disneyland Resort. The day culminates in a spectacular and patriotic firework display entitled "Disney's Celebrate America! A Fourth of July Concert in the Sky" in Disneyland Park. Over at Disney California Adventure, guests can expect World of Color to have an American themed pre-show.

This is one of the resort's busiest days of the year. Parks will fill to capacity early in the day which means that after a certain time no more guests will be allowed inside the theme parks for everyone's safety.

Wait times will be long for rides (so Fastpasses are definitely needed). If you exit the park, there is a chance you may not be re-admitted if it is full.

Disneyland Half Marathon – September 1st to September 4th 2016

Disneyland loves its puns, and therefore calls this "the happiest race of earth". The 13.1-mile route winds through the Disneyland Resort including both theme parks, and contains numerous photo opportunities along the way. As well as the half marathon, you can also take part in the Disneyland 10K, Dumbo Double Dare, Family Fun Run 5K and the Kids Races. As well as racing, there is an Expo and a Pasty Party too.

Disney's Halloween Season – Mid-September and all of October 2016

Disneyland's Halloween offers a "not so scary" alternative to what other theme parks such as Universal Studios Hollywood do. You will not find horror mazes or chainsaw-wielding maniacs here; instead be prepared to encounter the Disney villains who are out in full force. You can expect meet and greets with characters, a ghostly overlay at Space Mountain, a "Nightmare Before Christmas" overlay at the Haunted Mansion, pumpkin carving, and activities for the young ones too. Also, during much of the Halloween period, you can celebrate *Dia de Los Muertos* with a traditional skeleton display in Frontierland. Specific dates have not yet been announced for the 2016 season, but expect dates from mid-September through October 31st.

In addition, there is an extra hard-ticketed event **"Mickey's Halloween Party"** which takes place inside Disneyland Park. This party takes place on selected dates during the Halloween season and requires an extra ticket. On nights when there is a Halloween Party, the park closes early for regular guests. Party guests get to trick or treat around the park while enjoying select attractions, as well as getting to see the exclusive "Halloween Screams" fireworks display, cavalcades, take part in dance parties, explore candy trails, see lots of special entertainment and interact with characters. Party guests are exceptionally even allowed to dress up for the event.

For reference, 2015 party ticket prices were $69 to $84 each in advance, and $77 to $84 on the day of the event at the park gates. Tickets usually go on sale in late July. Expect these to be about $5 to $7 more expensive for 2016 dates.

Avengers Super Heroes Half Marathon – November 10th – 14th 2016
This Avengers 13.1-mile course is unique and different from the other marathons the resort offers throughout the year. As well as the half marathon, there is a 5K run, kids races, and an expo.

Chapter 19

Future Additions and a Special Thanks

Future Additions:

Star Wars Land Construction – Disneyland Resort is currently building a new Star Wars Land for the resort. This will be built in the former 'Big Thunder Ranch' area of Disneyland Park, near Big Thunder Mountain.

Star Wars Land will take guests to a never-before-seen planet. There will be two new major attractions: one will take guests on a secret mission on the Millennium Falcon, and the other puts them face-to-face with the First Order from "The Force Awakens".

This 14-acre land's construction begins in 2016 and there is no set opening date yet. We do not expect to see this open up before 2020 at the very earliest.

As part of this expansion numerous attractions are temporarily closed. These are: "Fantasmic!", Mark Twain Riverboat, Sailing Ship Columbia, Pirate's Lair on Tom Sawyer Island and Davy Crockett Explorer Canoes. These closed in January 2016 and no set re-opening date has yet been announced.

Soarin' Around the World – Disney has announced that 'Soarin' Over California' will become 'Soarin' Around the World' at some point during 2016. No longer will you only soar over California, but around the planet, as you see sights such as Monument Valley, the Great Wall of China, and many others. A date for this transition has not been given.

MagicBand/FastPass Tests – Walt Disney World has a digital FastPass system called FastPass+ that allows you to reserve Fastpasses digitally via your smartphone, an in-park kiosk or at home up to 60 days before arrival. In October 2015, Disneyland conducted a small-scale test where FastPasses began to be scanned at an attraction FastPass reader that strongly resembled those used in the Floridian system. We expect the Disneyland system to transition to be more similar to the Floridian version in the coming years.

Special Thanks:

If you have made it this far, thank you very much for reading everything. We hope this guide will make a big difference to your vacation, and that you have found tips that will save you time, money and hassle! Remember to take this guide with you while you are on vacation for the most enjoyment.

To contact us, use the form at www.independentguidebooks.com/contact-us/. If you have any corrections, feedback about any element of the guide, or a review of a ride or restaurant, send us a message and we will get back to you!

If you want to stay up to date check us out at **@IndepGuides** on Twitter and www.facebook.com/Independentguidebooks. We also encourage you to leave a review on Amazon or wherever you have purchased this guide from. Your reviews make a huge difference in helping other people find this guide. Thank you.

If you have enjoyed this guide, other travel guides in this series include:
- **The Independent Guide to Universal Studios Hollywood**
- **The Independent Guide to Universal Orlando**
- **The Independent Guide to Disneyland**
- **The Independent Guide to Walt Disney World**
- **The Independent Guide to Orlando**
- **The Independent Guide to Paris**
- **The Independent Guide to New York City**
- **The Independent Guide to London**

Have a magical stay!
P.S. Make sure to keep turning the pages to get to our exclusive in park maps which are just after the photo credits.

Photo credits:

The following photos have been used in this guide under a Creative Commons license. Thank you to:

AngryJulieMonday (Flickr user) for Tinker Bell Half Marathon; Anna Fox for Disneyland Railroad, Great Moments with Mr. Lincoln, Indiana Jones Adventure, Big Thunder Mountain Railroad, Star Tours, Fireworks, Animation Academy, Silly Symphony Swings, Lunar New Year, Holiday Season; Blake Handley for Paradise Pier Hotel; Christopher Paulin for Gadget's Go Coaster; Cliff Johnson for Astro Blasters; Derek Springer for Pirates of the Caribbean; Heather Harvey for Splash Mountain; Jack Miller for Downtown Disney; Jason Pratt for Toy Story Mania; Jeff Christiansen for Jumpin' Jellyfish; Joe Casabona for Tower of Terror; Josh Hallett for Soarin'; Justin Ennis for Dumbo and Space Mountain; Ken Lund for Radiator Springs Racers (cover); 'Marty the Adventurer' for the front cover image of Sleeping Beauty Castle; 'Prayitno' (Flickr user) for Grand Californian Hotel; Sam Howzit for Disneyland Hotel, Enchanted Tiki Room; and Tyler for California Screamin'.

Park Maps – Disneyland Park

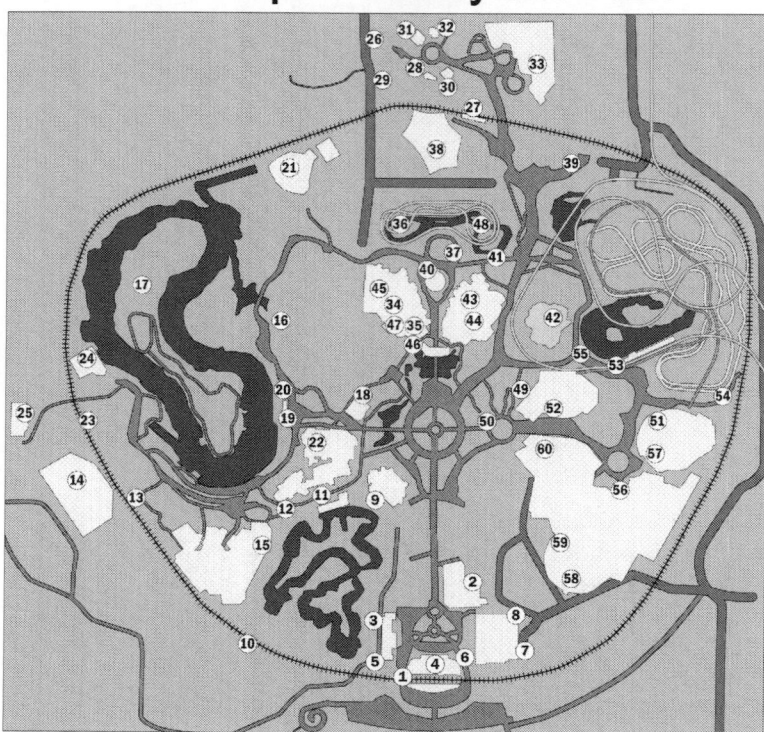

MAIN STREET USA
1. Disneyland Railroad
2. Main Street Cinema
3. Fire Engine
4. Horse-Drawn Streetcars
5. Horseless Carriag
6. Omnibus
7. The Disney Gallery
8. The Disneyland Story presenting Great Moments with Mr. Lincoln

ADVENTURELAND
9. Enchanted Tiki Room
10. Indiana Jones Adventure
11. Jungle Cruise
12. Tarzan's Treehouse

NEW ORLEANS SQUARE
13. Disneyland Railroad
14. Haunted Mansion
15. Pirates of the Caribbean

FRONTIERLAND
16. Big Thunder Mountain Railroad
17. Pirate's Lair Tom Sawyer Island
18. Frontierland Shootin' Exposition

19. Mark Twain Riverboat
20. Sailing Ship Columbia
21. Star Wars Land Construction
22. The Golden Horseshoe Stage

CRITTER COUNTRY
23. Splash Mountain
24. Davy Crockett's Explorer Canoes
25. The Many Adventures of Winnie The Pooh

MICKEY'S TOONTOWN
26. Chip 'n' Dale Treehouse
27. Disneyland Railroad
28. Donald's Boat
29. Gadget's Go Coaster
30. Goofy's Playhouse
31. Mickey's House & Meet Mickey
32. Minnie's House
33. Roger Rabbit's Car Toon Spin

FANTASYLAND
34. Alice in Wonderland
35. Bibbidi Bobbidi Boutique
36. Casy Jr. Circus Train
37. Dumbo the Flying Elephant
38. Fantasy Faire

39. "it's a small world"
40. King Arthur Carrousel
41. Mad Tea Party
42. Matterhorn Bobsleds
43. Mr. Toad's Wild Ride
44. Peter Pan's Flight
45. Pinocchio's Daring Journey
46. Sleeping Beauty Castle Walkthrough
47. Snow White's Scary Adventures
48. Storybook Land Canal Boats
49. Pixie Hollow

TOMORROWLAND
50. Astro Obitor
51. Autopia
52. Buzz Lightyear Astro Blasters
53. Disneyland Monorail
54. Disneyland Railroad
55. Finding Nemo Submarine Voyage
56. Tomorrowland Theater
57. Star Wars Launch Bay
58. Space Mountain
59. Starcade
60. Star Tours – The Adventures Continue

154

Disney California Adventure

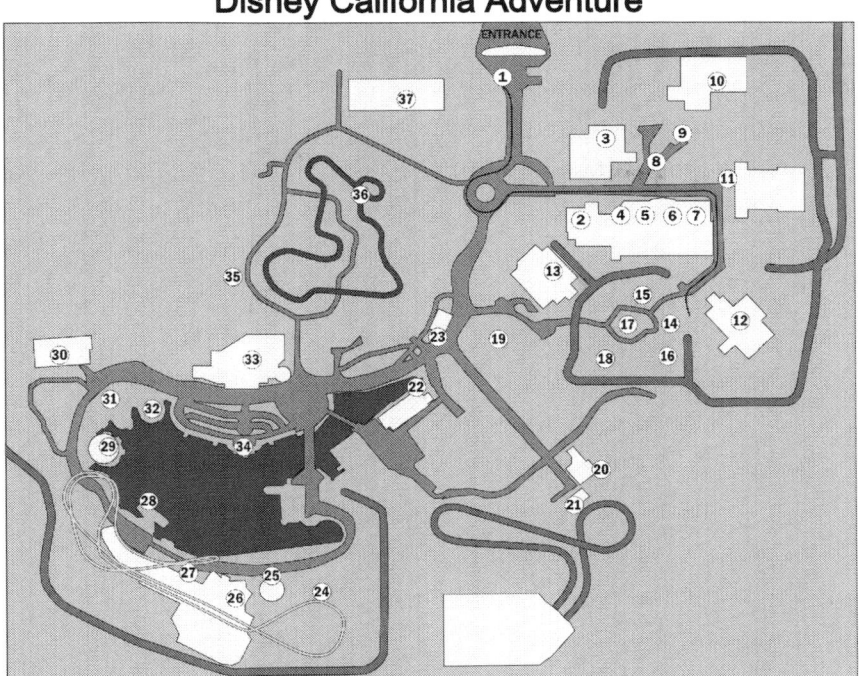

BUENA VISTA STREET
1. Red Car Trolley

HOLLYWOOD LAND
2. Disney Junior – Live on Stage!
3. Muppet*Vision 3D
4. Sorcerer's Workshop
5. Character Close-Up
6. Animation Academy
7. Turtle Talk with Crush
8. Red Car Trolley
9. The Hollywood Backlot Stage
10. Monsters, Inc. Mike & Sulley to the Rescue!
11. Frozen: Live at the Hyperion
12. The Twilight Zone: Tower of Terror

"A BUG'S LAND"
13. It's Tough to be a Bug!
14. Francis' Ladybug Boogie
15. Flik's Flyers
16. Tuck and Roll's Drive 'Em Buggies
17. Princess Dot Puddle Park
18. Heimlich's Chew Chew Train

CARS LAND
19. Mater's Junkyard Jamboree
20. Luigi's Rollickin' Roadsters
21. Radiator Springs Racers

PACIFIC WHARF
22. The Bakery Tour
23. Blue Sky Cellar

PARADISE PIER
24. California Screamin'
25. King Triton's Carousel
26. Toy Story Midway Mania!
27. Games of the Boardwalk
28. Mickey's Fun Wheel
29. Silly Symphony Swings
30. Goofy's Sky School
31. Jumping Jellyfish
32. Golden Zephyr
33. The Little Mermaid – Ariel's Undersea Adventure
34. World of Color

GRIZZLY PEAK
35. Redwood Creek Challenge Trail
36. Grizzly River Run
37. Soarin' Over California

Printed in Great Britain
by Amazon